BAINTE DEN STOC

WITHDRAWN FROM
DÚN LAOGHAIRE-RATHDOWN COUNTY
LIBRARY STOCK

D0246846

Keeping it Simple

Keeping it Simple

Derry Clarke

GILL & MACMILLAN

Gill & Macmillan Ltd
Hume Avenue, Park West, Dublin 12
with associated companies throughout the world
www.gillmacmillan.ie

© Derry Clarke 2009
978 07171 4619 2

Index compiled by Cover to Cover
Design and typesetting by Anú Design, Tara
Printed by and bound by Oriental Press, Dubai

This book is typeset in 10pt Franklin Gothic on 16pt.

The paper used in this book comes from the wood pulp of managed forests.
For every tree felled, at least one tree is planted, thereby renewing natural resources.

All rights reserved.
No part of this publication may be copied, reproduced or transmitted
in any form or by any means without written permission of the publishers.

A CIP catalogue record for this book is available from the British Library.

5 4 3 2 1

Dedicated to

Sallyanne

Contents

5   Fish

6 Dessert

Acknowledgments

I would like to start by thanking everyone involved in this project, without whose hard work and dedication it would not have been possible. Mary Wedick is at the very top of my list: her unfailing help, patience and support were invaluable. Chefs Rory Carville, Sandy Sabek and Joyce O'Sullivan were great back-up support – the girls especially where desserts were concerned. Thank you all so very much. Thank you to Ronan Lange for his excellent photography – his patience and support are so very much appreciated; to Sarah Liddy and all her team at Gill & Macmillan; and to Noel Kelly and Niamh Kirwan at N.K. Management. Last and not least, to my lovely wife, Sallyanne.

Conversion charts

Note: All equivalents are approximate. Use either metric or imperial measures; never mix the two.

Weight		Volume		Oven Temperatures			
				Degrees Celsius	Degrees Fahrenheit	Gas Mark	Description
10g	½oz	5ml	1 teaspoon	110	225	¼	Cool
20g	¾oz	10ml	1 dessertspoon	120/130	250	½	Cool
25g	1oz	15ml	1 tablespoon	140	275	1	Very low
50g	2oz	30ml	1 fl oz	150	300	2	Very low
60g	2½oz	50ml	2 fl oz	160/170	325	3	Low
75g	3oz	75ml	2½ fl oz	180	350	4	Moderate
100g	3½oz	100ml	3 fl oz	190	375	5	Moderately hot
110g	4oz	125ml	4 fl oz	200	400	6	Hot
150g	5oz	150ml	5 fl oz (¼ pint)	220	425	7	Hot
175g	6oz	200ml	7 fl oz (½ pint)	230	450	8	Very hot
200g	7oz	250ml	9 fl oz	250	475	9	Very hot
225g	8oz	300ml	10 fl oz				
250g	9oz	350ml	12 fl oz				
275g	10oz	400ml	14 fl oz				
350g	12oz	425ml	15 fl oz (¾ pint)				
400g	14oz	475ml	16 fl oz				
450g	1lb	500ml	18 fl oz				
500g	18oz	600ml	1 pint				
600g	1¼lb	700ml	1¼ pints				
700g	1½lb	850 ml	1½ pints				
900g	2lb	1 litre	1¾ pints				
1kg	2¼lb	1.2 litres	2 pints				
1.1kg	2½lb	1.5 litres	2½ pints				
1.3kg	3lb	1.8 litres	3 pints				
1.5kg	3lb 5oz	2 litres	3½ pints				
1.6kg	3½lb						
1.8kg	4lb						
2kg	4½lb						
2.2kg	5lb						

Introduction

'Food, glorious food!' That is the ethos I grew up with. My father – D. J. Clarke of John Clarke and Sons – was a food importer, and my mother's father, Nicholas McEvoy, was a fruit importer for Connolly Shaw. Any new produce or new lines were brought home from both sources and we got to taste them. This gave me the interest in all food that I still have today. I am never afraid to try anything new or different where food is concerned.

L'Ecrivain Restaurant is twenty years old this year. We have come a long way in that time. Ireland and its producers, particularly indigenous, local and organic producers, are much more to the forefront than they were all those years ago. There were no such luxuries as farmers' markets, at least not as many as there are today. Fish suppliers practically gave away monkfish in those days just to get rid of it. Now it is a very expensive and sought-after fish. Times have indeed changed.

All this has given me a healthy respect, not just for the end result, but also for the producers, distributors and eventual sellers of food. To be a good cook, you need at least a basic knowledge of the foods you are preparing. Knowing their source and their season is very important. Cooking foods in season makes all the difference to the flavours.

My menus in the restaurant are always seasonal – this ensures you are getting the product at its best. The constant changes keep me and my team on our toes – and we would get bored if we cooked the same things day in, day out. I admire chefs who have the same menu all the time, because I would find this type of cooking extremely difficult. I am always looking for new ways of cooking and presenting old faithfuls – especially now.

The last cookbook I wrote, with my wife Sallyanne, was a reflection of l'Ecrivain and of the recipes that are used in the restaurant, the team who work with us, our suppliers and our customers.

Keeping It Simple has recipes that anyone can use. The recipes are simple and straightforward, and the ingredients are accessible and affordable. I have tried to present them so that they are easy to follow – I hope you agree. Remember, recipes are a guide – don't be a slave to them. Never be afraid to add your own individual elements to make them your own.

Preparation is the key to anything in life, especially cooking. Make out your shopping list in advance. Check your larder and bin anything out of date. Prepare as much as possible beforehand and enjoy the food you prepare. Lots of these recipes are ideal for lunch/dinner parties. Make it fun and cook from the heart. Most of all, my wish is that you will use and enjoy this book.

Note: all the recipes in this book, except where otherwise indicated, serve four people.

1

Roast pumpkin soup with coconut milk · Roast red pepper soup with
chorizo and white beans · Spiced parsnip and apple cider velouté with
seared scallops · Cream of spinach soup with nutmeg and poached egg ·
Roast pumpkin soup with coconut milk · Roast red pepper soup with chorizo and
white beans · Spiced parsnip and apple cider velouté with seared scallops · Cream of spinach soup with nutmeg
and poached egg · Roast pumpkin soup with coconut milk · Roast red pepper soup with chorizo and white beans
· Spiced parsnip and apple cider velouté with seared scallops · Cream of spinach soup with nutmeg and poached
egg · Roast pumpkin soup with coconut milk · Roast red pepper soup with chorizo and white beans · Spiced
parsnip and apple cider velouté with seared scallops · Cream of spinach soup with nutmeg and poached egg

Soups

Roast pumpkin soup with coconut milk

In the past, pumpkins were rarely used in Irish cooking. I think they are a welcome introduction. The coconut milk in this soup gives a great flavour to the pumpkin, which could otherwise be slightly bland.

1 pumpkin, about 1.5kg
1 tablespoon chopped sage
1 tablespoon chopped thyme
2 onions (sliced)
1 thumb-sized piece root ginger (peeled)
2 cloves garlic (crushed)
2 teaspoons curry spices
1 tablespoons brown sugar
1 litre chicken stock
200ml coconut milk
cream (optional)

1. Preheat the oven to 170˚C.
2. Cut the pumpkin in half and bake in the oven with the sage and thyme until soft (about an hour). Allow to cool and remove the flesh.
3. Slowly sweat the onion, ginger and garlic in a large pot for 10 minutes.
4. Add the spices, pumpkin and sugar.
5. Cook gently for 5 minutes and then add the chicken stock.
6. Simmer gently for 30–40 minutes.
7. Season and add the coconut milk, and a little cream if desired. Warm through.

Roast red pepper soup
with chorizo and white beans

I cannot emphasise enough how easy you will find this soup to make. When you have tried this recipe, you will see how much better it is to make your own soup rather than buy it ready made. Use really good-quality peppers and tomatoes.

4 red peppers (halved and
    deseeded)
6 plum tomatoes (skinned
    and deseeded)
2 tablespoons olive oil, plus
    extra to serve
1 onion (diced)
1 clove garlic (crushed)
1 chilli (diced and deseeded)
1 carrot (peeled and diced)
1 stick celery (diced)
1 tablespoon tomato paste
1 litre hot chicken stock
1 tablespoon white wine vinegar
4 tablespoons cooked
    white beans
4 tablespoons diced chorizo
basil leaves, to garnish

1. Preheat the oven to 180°C.
2. Place the peppers and tomatoes in a roasting tray, drizzle with olive oil and roast for 25 minutes. When they have cooled, remove the skins.
3. Heat the olive oil in a large saucepan and cook the onion, garlic and chilli until soft.
4. Add the peppers, tomato, carrot and celery, and cook gently for 3 minutes.
5. Add the tomato paste, chicken stock and vinegar and simmer for 30 minutes.
6. Liquidise and season to taste.
7. Add the beans and chorizo.

To serve:

1. Serve the soup in four warmed bowls with some basil leaves and drizzle with olive oil.

Spiced parsnip and apple cider velouté with seared scallops

The trick when cooking scallops is to be very careful not to overcook them, which makes them tough. Anything sweet works well with scallops, and parsnip and apple always work well together.

For the velouté

½ onion (diced)

1 clove garlic (crushed)

1 teaspoon chopped fresh ginger

200g butter

4 parsnips (peeled and chopped)

2 eating apples (peeled and chopped)

2 teaspoons curry paste or powder (use more if you like more heat)

½ litre chicken or vegetable stock

150ml cider

For the scallops

8 large scallops (shelled and roe removed)

4 slices Parma ham

For the velouté

1. Sweat the onion, garlic and ginger in the butter for 1 minute.
2. Add the parsnip and apple and cook for a further 1 minute.
3. Add the curry paste or powder and cook for 1 minute.
4. Add the stock, season with salt and pepper and allow to simmer for 20 minutes.
5. Add the cider, liquidise and pass through a sieve.

For the scallops

1. Cut the scallops in half and sear them on a hot oiled non-stick pan for 30 seconds on each side.
2. Take two baking trays and lay the slices of Parma ham flat on one.
3. Place the second baking tray, base down, on top of the Parma ham.
4. Bake at 180°C for 10 minutes, until crisp.

To serve

1. Pour the velouté into four warmed shallow soup bowls. Place the scallops in the centre with the Parma ham.
2. Serve with crusty white bread.

Cream of spinach soup
with nutmeg and poached egg

The trick with this dish is not to add the spinach too early. If the spinach is cooked too long, it will lose its wonderful green colour and turn greyish. You want to keep all the vibrance of the fresh leaves. If the soup is not as green as you would like, add some more spinach towards the end of the cooking time. As an alternative to the poached egg, you could serve some garlic croûtons with the soup.

4 eggs (for poaching)

2 onions (sliced)

4 potatoes (peeled and diced)

2 cloves garlic (crushed)

100g butter

200g fresh spinach leaves

1 teaspoon nutmeg (freshly grated)

1 litre chicken stock

200ml cream

For the poached eggs

1. Bring a large saucepan of salted water to simmering point.
2. Gently break the eggs into the saucepan, one at a time.
3. Cook for 1 minute, then take the saucepan off the heat.
4. Allow the eggs to sit in the water for 6 minutes. This gives a translucent egg with a soft, creamy yolk.
5. Remove the eggs with a slotted spoon.

For the soup

1. Slowly sweat the onion, potato and garlic in the butter for 10 minutes.
2. Add the spinach, nutmeg and chicken stock.
3. Bring to the boil and simmer for 20 minutes.
4. Liquidise and add the cream.
5. Serve with poached egg and a little grated nutmeg.

2

Salads

Carpaccio of beef with salad and horseradish mayonnaise

Carpaccio of beef is surprisingly popular in the restaurant. The thinner you can slice the beef, the better. In this recipe, it's served with Gabriel cheese, which is a lovely mature hard cheese from west Cork.

400g beef fillet (trimmed of
  all fat)
1 tablespoon Dijon mustard
1 tablespoon black peppercorns (crushed)
1 tablespoon sea salt
1 tablespoon chopped parsley

For the cheese and watercress salad

1 bunch watercress (washed)
1 tablespoon horseradish
  mixed with the juice of
  1 lemon
1 cup mayonnaise
200g Gabriel cheese or
  Parmesan

1. Rub the beef on all sides with the mustard.
2. Mix the crushed peppercorns, salt and parsley and roll the beef in the mixture.
3. Roll tightly in clingfilm and place in the freezer for 6 hours or until frozen.
4. Slice very thinly with a very sharp carving knife.

To serve

1. Lay the beef on a plate, arrange the watercress on top and season with sea salt and pepper.
2. Mix the horseradish with the mayonnaise.
3. Grate the cheese over the salad and serve the mayonnaise on the side.

Caesar salad

This is possibly one of the most popular salads of all, but also one of the most abused, with many odd combinations that really don't work. I think this classic Caesar salad is the best.

1 head cos lettuce

For the dressing
100g aged Parmesan cheese
   (grated)
200ml mayonnaise
100g anchovies (finely chopped)

For the croûtons and Parma ham
½ stick French bread
4 cloves garlic (sliced)
1 tablespoon chopped thyme
olive oil
4 slices Parma ham

To dress the salad
100g anchovies (whole)
200g aged Parmesan cheese
   (shaved)
150ml olive oil

For the dressing
1. Mix the grated Parmesan, mayonnaise and anchovies to make a smooth dressing.

For the croûtons and Parma ham
1. Preheat the oven to 180˚C.
2. Slice the bread and place on a baking tray.
3. Sprinkle with the garlic, thyme and olive oil.
4. Season with sea salt and black pepper.
5. Place in the oven and bake for 10 minutes.
6. Take two baking trays and lay the slices of Parma ham flat on one.
7. Place the second baking tray, base down, on top of the Parma ham.
8. Bake at 180˚C for 10 minutes, until crisp.

To assemble
1. Wash the lettuce and toss in the dressing.
2. Add the whole anchovies, croûtons, Parmesan and Parma ham.
3. Drizzle with the olive oil.

Chicory salad with chestnut dressing

Chicory, also known as endives, is not seen too often these days, but I love it. It has a deliciously bitter, tangy taste and a lovely crunchy texture which is great in salads. The Brussels sprout leaves add a fantastic peppery flavour to this dish, making it a wonderful wintery salad.

4 heads chicory (washed)

150g green beans (blanched)

100g Brussels sprout leaves (leaves separated and blanched in boiling water for 30 seconds, then refreshed in cold water)

100g bean sprouts

For the chestnut dressing

2 cups cooked chestnuts (chopped)

2 shallots (diced)

1 cup chervil (chopped)

1 teaspoon Dijon mustard

2 tablespoons balsamic vinegar

1 cup olive oil

1. Arrange the chicory, green beans, Brussels sprout leaves and bean sprouts on a large plate.
2. Mix all the dressing ingredients and pour over the salad.
3. Season with salt and pepper.

Pheasant, spiced apple and parsnip Waldorf salad

Cook the pheasant on the bone, as this will give extra flavour to the meat. Pheasant is often farmed these days, and it is not as well flavoured as wild pheasant. Draping streaky bacon over the pheasant during cooking will help make the meat more flavoursome.

1 pheasant crown

4 green apples

50g celeriac batons

20g celery (diced)

10g walnuts

100g pancetta (diced)

50ml walnut oil

200g parsnip (peeled and chopped)

a little butter

1 tablespoon curry powder

100ml chicken stock

1. Lightly season the pheasant and roast in a preheated oven at 180°C for 45 minutes to an hour.
2. Core and slice two of the apples and mix with the celeriac, celery, walnuts and diced pancetta in a bowl.
3. Toss with the walnut oil and set aside.
4. Peel, core and dice the other two apples.
5. Sweat the parsnip in the butter in a large pan. Add the curry powder and the diced apple. Add the chicken stock and continue to cook until the parsnip and apple are soft.
6. When cooked, purée the parsnip and apple mixture.

To serve

1. Carve the pheasant. Arrange the meat on the Waldorf salad.
2. Spoon the purée onto the plate.

Salad of field mushrooms with rocket, chorizo and fried egg

Mushroom is one of my favourite flavours. Chorizo and rocket served with mushrooms gives a great plateful of contrasting flavours. For a healthier option, poach the egg instead of frying it. To make this a vegetarian dish, omit the chorizo.

4 large flat cap mushrooms
  (cleaned)
1 tablespoon Worcestershire
  sauce
juice of 1 lemon
50g butter, plus extra for frying
  the eggs
200g chorizo (sliced)
4 free-range eggs
1 large bunch fresh rocket
  (washed)

For the dressing

100ml extra virgin olive oil
25ml English mustard
25ml sherry vinegar
1 tablespoon chopped fresh
  parsley

1. Place the mushrooms on a flat tray, drizzle with the Worcestershire sauce and lemon juice and dot with the butter.
2. Season with black pepper and grill under a high heat for 2 minutes.
3. Add the chorizo and cook for a further 2–3 minutes.
4. Fry the eggs in a little butter in a heavy frying pan until cooked.

For the dressing

1. Mix all the ingredients together.

To assemble

1. Place the mushrooms on the centre of a plate with the rocket leaves, place the eggs on top and drizzle with the dressing.

Warm salad of lamb's liver, crispy bacon and garlic potatoes

Lamb's liver is a very popular lunch dish. It is reasonably priced and is really underused, but the combination of bacon and liver is so tasty. You could substitute the garlic potatoes with mashed potato and sautéed onion. Veal liver, which is a lot more expensive, could be used instead of lamb's liver.

500g sliced lamb's liver
vegetable oil
4 cured back rashers
2 potatoes (peeled and diced)
2 cloves garlic (chopped)
200ml olive oil
2 tablespoons chopped chives
2 cupfuls lamb's lettuce (mache)
1 bunch chives
4 bunches watercress

For the dressing

100ml Dijon mustard
50ml honey or maple syrup
20ml white wine vinegar

1. Sear the liver in a hot pan with a little vegetable oil.
2. Cook for 2 minutes on each side and season. Keep warm.
3. Under a hot grill, cook the bacon until crisp.
4. In a pan, toss the potatoes in the garlic and olive oil.
5. When the potatoes are tender and browned all over, add the chopped chives and season.

For the dressing

1. In a bowl, mix together the mustard, honey and vinegar.

To assemble

1. Arrange the liver and bacon in the centre of a plate.
2. Surround with the lamb's lettuce, chives and watercress.
3. Scatter the potatoes over the salad and drizzle with the dressing.

ow-roasted butternut squash with goat's cheese   •   Gnocchi with
rusalem artichoke and pickled mushrooms   •   Green asparagus spears
th oven-dried tomatoes and spicy root vegetable and black olive dressing   •
oat's cheese tartlets with aubergine caviar   •   Honey-roasted vegetables with mustard mayonnaise   •   Warm baby
egetables with crispy capers   •   Slow-roasted butternut squash with goat's cheese   •   Gnocchi with Jerusalem
tichoke and pickled mushrooms·   •   Green asparagus spears with oven-dried tomatoes and spicy root vegetable and
ack olive dressing   •   Goat's cheese tartlets with aubergine caviar   •   Honey-roasted vegetables with mustard
ayonnaise   •   Warm baby vegetables with crispy capers   •   Slow-roasted butternut squash with goat's cheese   •
nocchi with Jerusalem artichoke and pickled mushrooms   •   Honey-roasted vegetables with mustard mayonnaise

3

Vegetarian

Slow-roasted butternut squash with goat's cheese

While goat's cheese is often featured on vegetarian menus, this dish gives it an interesting twist. The sage releases a great flavour with the goat's cheese. Slow roasting the butternut squash ensures it tastes fantastic. You could use your own choice of nuts or seeds instead of the pine nuts.

For the squash

2 butternut squash
2 tablespoons chopped sage
2 tablespoons honey
2 tablespoons olive oil
4 cloves garlic (sliced)

For the goat's cheese

200g goat's cheese
100g toasted pine nuts
1 tablespoon chopped sage

rocket, to garnish

For the squash

1. Cut the squash in half lengthways.
2. Remove the seeds and coat with the sage, honey, olive oil and garlic.
3. Season with sea salt and freshly ground black pepper.
4. Place in a preheated oven at 160°C for 1 hour until tender.
5. Remove and set aside.

For the goat's cheese

1. Crumble the goat's cheese, mix with the pine nuts and sage and place in the hollows of the squash.
2. Bake in the oven for 5 minutes at 180°C, until the cheese has melted.
3. Garnish with some rocket and serve with a salad.

Gnocchi with Jerusalem artichoke and pickled mushrooms

Gnocchi features quite often on vegetarian menus, but you need to choose carefully what you serve with the gnocchi, as it can be slightly bland. This recipe uses pickled mushrooms, packed full of strong flavours. Jerusalem artichoke is a delicious but underrated vegetable that should be used more often.

For the gnocchi

200g flour
200g warm baked potato flesh (mashed)
2 small or 1½ large eggs
50g grated Parmesan cheese
2 tablespoons chopped parsley

For the artichokes

500g Jerusalem artichokes
1 litre milk
1 sprig thyme
1 clove garlic

For the mushrooms

50g girolle mushrooms
50g trompette mushrooms
50g ceps
50g portobello mushrooms
50ml olive oil
10ml Chardonnay vinegar
1 tablespoon fresh chopped tarragon

For the gnocchi

1. Sift the flour into a large bowl.
2. Add the potato, then the egg, cheese and parsley.
3. Season the mix and form into a soft dough.
4. Divide the mixture into quarters and roll each quarter into a cylindrical shape.
5. Divide each cylinder into 5 pieces. Lightly press a fork into the top of each piece.
6. Cook the gnocchi in batches in boiling salted water for 5 minutes. The gnocchi are cooked when they rise to the top. They are now ready to serve, or you could brown them on a pan in a little oil for a different texture.

For the artichokes

1. Peel the artichokes and put them in a saucepan with the milk, thyme and garlic.
2. Season and simmer until tender.
3. Remove from the milk.

For the mushrooms

1. Clean and trim all the mushrooms and sauté in a pan with the olive oil, vinegar and tarragon.

Green asparagus spears with oven-dried tomatoes and spicy root vegetable and black olive dressing

Green asparagus should only ever be used when in season. Never overcook it, as this completely ruins it. Asparagus is traditionally served with hollandaise sauce, but this recipe is a different, lighter way to serve it.

16 green asparagus spears
  (peeled and trimmed)

For the tomatoes

4 plum tomatoes
a little thyme (chopped)
a little garlic (chopped)

For the spicy root vegetable and black olive dressing

1 carrot
1 stick celery
1 small fennel bulb
1 red onion
1 teaspoon curry paste or
  red Thai curry paste
1 tablespoon olive oil
1 bunch coriander (chopped)
juice of 1 lime
8 pitted black olives

1. Slice the tomatoes and cook them in a low oven (60°C) with a little chopped thyme and garlic for 2–3 hours.
2. Finely dice the carrot, celery, fennel and onion.
3. Mix together the curry paste, olive oil, coriander and lime juice.
4. Add the root vegetables and olives.
5. Lightly season and chill.

To serve

1. Boil or steam the asparagus spears until tender, about 5–7 minutes (do not overcook).
2. Place the tomatoes on a plate, then place the asparagus on top. Pour over the dressing.

Goat's cheese tartlets with aubergine caviar

Goat's cheese is a popular, tasty cheese, and melting it really brings out its flavour. In a recipe with so few ingredients, it's very important to ensure that you use the best quality ingredients you can. Aubergine caviar sounds a lot more impressive than aubergine purée!

For the tartlets

4 plum tomatoes
4 rounds puff pastry
    (each 8cm in diameter)
    (recipe on p. 160)
200g goat's cheese, cut into
    4 equal portions
1 tablespoon chopped thyme

For the aubergine caviar

1 large aubergine (halved
    lengthways)
1 tomato (halved and deseeded)
1 tablespoon balsamic vinegar
1 tablespoon olive oil
1 bay leaf

For the tartlets

1. First skin the tomatoes. Plunge them into hot water for about 1½ minutes, then refresh with cold water – this will make the skins come off more easily. Slice the skinned tomatoes.
2. Take the rounds of pastry and divide the sliced tomato equally between them. Put 1 portion of goat's cheese on each pastry round.
3. Season with sea salt, pepper and chopped thyme.
4. Bake in a preheated oven at 190˚C for 6 minutes.

For the aubergine caviar

1. Place the aubergine on a roasting tray, cut halves facing up, with the tomato, balsamic vinegar, olive oil and bay leaf.
2. Season with sea salt and pepper.
3. Bake in a preheated oven at 120˚C for 1 hour.
4. Remove from the oven and allow to cool.
5. Scrape all the flesh from the cooled aubergine, then chop finely and mix with the tomato and any juice from the tray.
6. Serve the aubergine caviar over or alongside the tarts.

Honey-roasted vegetables with mustard mayonnaise

What I love about this dish is that it can be served as an accompaniment to a meat dish or on its own as a vegetarian main course. It is lovely and colourful, and packed full of flavours. You can substitute any of the vegetables I have used with your own favourites.

100g butter

1 tablespoon olive oil

8 baby carrots (peeled)

2 red onions (quartered)

4 shallots (halved)

2 small onions (halved)

1 bulb garlic (halved horizontally)

1 aubergine (sliced)

2 courgettes (sliced)

200ml honey

juice of 1 lime

juice of 1 lemon

2 tablespoons balsamic vinegar

1 tablespoon chopped thyme

2 tablespoons brown sugar

4 spring onions (chopped)

For the mustard mayonnaise

200ml mayonnaise

2 tablespoons Dijon mustard

1. To make the mustard mayonnaise, simply mix together the mayonnaise and mustard.
2. Melt the butter with the olive oil in a large frying pan.
3. Add all the vegetables and cook until browned, about 5 minutes.
4. Add the honey, lime juice, lemon juice, vinegar, thyme and sugar.
5. Cook for 10–15 minutes.
6. Garnish with spring onion to serve.

Warm baby vegetables with crispy capers

This salad looks fantastic when served in a large glass bowl in the centre of the table. It can be served as a starter, either on its own or with creamy dips. Any seasonal vegetables can be used in this recipe in place of the baby vegetables.

100ml extra virgin olive oil

1 piece ginger, about twice the size of your thumb (peeled and sliced)

2 red chillies (deseeded and diced)

100g baby carrots (peeled and blanched)

100g baby beetroot (peeled and blanched)

100g turnip (peeled and blanched)

100g courgettes (peeled and blanched)

100g leeks (peeled and blanched)

100ml white wine vinegar

4 spring onions (sliced)

100g capers

selection of cress (watercress, mustard cress and baby cress)

For the warm baby vegetables

1. In a wok or a large saucepan, warm the olive oil, add the ginger and chillies and cook for 2 minutes over a medium heat.

2. Add the vegetables, heat through and add the wine vinegar and spring onions.

3. Fry the capers until crisp and sprinkle over the salad.

4

Meat, Poultry and Game

Whole chicken, spicy, sweet and sour

Roast chicken can be a little boring, but roasting it this way not only gives it a spicy flavour, but makes the chicken look great too. If you prefer, you could use four chicken breasts and finish them off in the pan. As an alternative to roast potatoes, you could serve some pan-fried noodles.

1 whole chicken (not too big: about 1.3–1.8kg or 3–4lb)

For the paste

2 red chillies (deseeded and chopped)

2 tablespoons curry powder or any spice mix

50g ginger (chopped)

6 cloves garlic (chopped)

2 tablespoons brown sugar

2 tablespoon chopped thyme

1 tablespoon chopped sage

1 tablespoon sea salt

3 tablespoons olive oil

2 tablespoons white wine vinegar

1. Mix together all the paste ingredients except the oil and vinegar.
2. Rub the chicken with the olive oil and vinegar and sprinkle the dry mixture over the chicken.
3. Season with some freshly ground black pepper.
4. Preheat the oven to 190˚C and roast the chicken for about 2 hours (30–35 minutes per 500g/25–30 minutes per pound), basting frequently.
5. Allow to rest for 10 minutes before carving.

Crispy duck breast
with glazed butternut squash

Before cooking duck breast, rub the skin with sea salt for extra crispness. Cooking the duck skin side down in a pan that you heat from cold also helps the skin to cook through. I would recommend serving duck pink. The butternut squash in this dish cuts the richness of the duck.

4 duck breasts
1 large bunch of rocket leaves
olive oil

For the glazed butternut squash

1 butternut squash (peeled
    and cubed)
4 large shallots (halved)
200g cured bacon (blanched
    and cubed)
juice of 1 orange
juice of 1 lime
1 tablespoon olive oil
1 tablespoon honey
50g butter
50g chopped fresh sage
50g chopped fresh thyme

For the glazed butternut squash

1. Place the butternut squash, shallots and bacon in a bowl. Add the orange and lime juice, olive oil, honey, butter, sage and thyme.
2. Season with sea salt and cracked black pepper.
3. Toss all the ingredients together and spread on a roasting tray.
4. Bake in a preheated oven at 180°C until tender, about 15–20 minutes.

For the duck

1. Place the duck breasts skin side down on a cold heavy frying pan.
2. Cook on a high heat until the skin is crisp (about 5 minutes).
3. Turn the breasts over and reduce the heat.
4. Cook for a further 3–5 minutes for pink, longer for medium or well done.

To serve

1. Allow the duck breasts to rest.
2. Carve the breasts lengthways.
3. Spoon the squash onto serving plates, place the duck on top with the rocket leaves, and drizzle with olive oil.

Roast crispy duck with orange and star anise

Serving a whole duck at the table looks very impressive. Carve at the table by first removing the legs, then carving the breast. Orange and star anise really works with duck.

4 oranges

1 bunch thyme

1 duck, about 1.5–2kg

2 tablespoons sea salt

65g brown sugar

100ml red wine vinegar

1 tablespoon star anise

2 cups gravy (stock cube or granules will do fine)

1. Zest and squeeze the oranges, retaining the husks.
2. Put the husks of orange and the thyme into the cavity of the duck.
3. Rub the sea salt into the skin.
4. Preheat the oven to 170˚C. Place the duck on a wire rack in a deep roasting tray and roast in the oven for about 1½ hours.
5. Leave to rest for 10 minutes before carving.

For the sauce

1. Heat the sugar in a saucepan until it forms a brown caramel.
2. Add the vinegar and simmer over a low heat.
3. When the mixture starts to caramelise, add the orange juice, star anise and gravy.
4. Simmer until the sauce reaches the desired thickness, then strain, season and add the orange zest.

Roast wood pigeon with smoked bacon in sherry, beetroot and grapes

If you haven't yet tried it, wood pigeon is definitely worth a go, and it is readily available in season. Sherry really contributes a lot to the taste of this recipe, which is quite a sophisticated winter dinner party dish.

4 wood pigeons (oven ready)
1 tablespoon vegetable oil

For the smoked bacon in sherry, beetroot and grapes

2 shallots (diced)
1 clove garlic (crushed)
200g smoked bacon (diced)
2 beetroot (peeled and diced)
100ml sweet sherry
200ml stock (beef or granules)
2 bay leaves
100g black or green grapes
    (halved and deseeded)
parsley, chives or chervil, to
    garnish

1. Heat the vegetable oil in a hot pan and seal the pigeon on all sides.
2. Season with sea salt and freshly ground black pepper.
3. Place in an ovenproof dish with a lid.

For the smoked bacon in sherry, beetroot and grape

1. In the same pan in which you sealed the pigeon, sauté the shallots and garlic for 2 minutes.
2. Add the bacon and beetroot and sauté for 2 minutes.
3. Add the sherry and simmer for a further 2 minutes.
4. Add the stock.
5. Pour the mixture over the pigeon and add the bay leaves.
6. Cover the dish with a lid and roast in a preheated oven at 180°C for 1 hour.
7. Remove the pigeons and add the grapes to the sauce.
8. Check the seasoning and pour the sauce over the pigeon.
9. Garnish with chopped herbs.

Spiced pot roasted partridge with carrot, apple and Puy lentils

A partridge is smaller than a chicken, but when cooking partridge you can just treat the bird as you would a chicken. Partridge is really tasty, a little lighter in flavour than pheasant. This is a good dish to try if you are new to cooking game.

4 oven-ready partridge

1 tablespoon vegetable oil

1 tablespoon curry spices or curry powder

1 tablespoon chopped thyme

4 shallots

100g cured bacon (diced)

1 clove garlic (crushed)

2 carrots (peeled and cut into large dice)

vegetable oil

400ml chicken stock

1 glass sherry vinegar

2 bay leaves

150g Puy lentils (cooked)

2 apples (peeled, cored and diced)

1 tablespoon chopped parsley, to garnish

1. Coat the partridge with the oil and sprinkle with the spices and thyme.
2. Season with sea salt and freshly ground black pepper.
3. In a hot pan, seal the partridge on all sides and place in a deep ovenproof dish with a lid.
4. Sauté the shallots, bacon, garlic, and carrots in a little vegetable oil for 3 minutes.
5. Add the chicken stock, vinegar and bay leaves, then add the lentils.
6. Pour over the partridge, cover and bake in the oven at 180°C for 20–25 minutes.
7. Add the diced apple.
8. Garnish with the chopped parsley.

Pot roasted breast of chicken with garlic and herbs

Chicken does need a little help with flavour. Roasting the chicken with garlic and sherry vinegar, all in the one pot, means that the chicken takes on some wonderful flavours. Don't be put off by the quantity of garlic in the ingredients: the flavour breaks down during cooking and leaves a wonderful taste that is not overpowering at all.

12 pearl (pickling) onions (peeled)

2 tablespoons olive oil

4 chicken breasts (skin on)

24 cloves garlic (peeled)

1 tablespoon chopped thyme

1 tablespoon chopped rosemary

25g brown sugar

4 bay leaves

1 tablespoon chopped sage

1 tablespoon chopped chives

2 tablespoons sherry vinegar

1. Put the onions in a saucepan of boiling water, simmer for 5 minutes and refresh under cold running water.

2. Heat the olive oil in a heavy pan and brown the chicken breasts on both sides.

3. Add the garlic, onions, thyme, rosemary and sugar.

4. Cook for 2 minutes and season, then place in an earthenware dish, add the bay leaves, cover the dish and bake in a preheated oven for 30 minutes at 180˚C.

5. Five minutes before the end of the cooking time, add the sage, chives and sherry vinegar.

Pheasant roasted with smoked bacon and sage, with red cabbage salad

It's becoming harder and harder to source wild pheasant, which is very reasonably priced when in season (October to January). While farmed pheasant is readily available, it is not as flavoursome as the wild bird. Red cabbage is great with game. In this dish, the red cabbage is used in a salad for a lighter meal, but you could also serve it with slowly braised red cabbage.

4 oven-ready pheasants

250g cured bacon (cut into large dice)

1 onion (sliced)

2 cloves garlic (sliced)

150ml red wine

100ml stock (chicken) – stock made with a cube is fine

1 bunch sage (chopped)

2 bay leaves

For the red cabbage salad

1¼ head red cabbage (finely shredded)

1 green apple (cored and finely sliced)

2 tablespoons raisins or sultanas

100ml balsamic vinegar

2 tablespoons olive oil

2 tablespoons chopped chives

For the pheasant

1. Brown and seal the pheasants in a hot oiled pan.
2. Season and place in an ovenproof dish.
3. Put the bacon, onion and garlic in the pan and sauté for 2–4 minutes.
4. Add to the pheasants in the ovenproof dish.
5. Pour the wine and stock into the pan and add the sage and bay leaves.
6. Simmer for 2 minutes, then add to the pheasant.
7. Cover the dish and bake in the oven at 170°C for 1 hour.
8. Remove the pheasants and strain the liquid into a saucepan.
9. Boil the liquid until it is reduced by half.

For the red cabbage salad

1. Toss all the ingredients together in a bowl and season.

Lamb's kidneys with pickled gherkin, tomato and basil

I probably wouldn't recommend this as a dinner party dish, as a lot of people won't eat kidneys. They are delicious when cooked correctly: do not overcook them, as this makes them very dry. The gherkin and tomato add a sharp, tangy flavour, and tomato and basil is a proven combination. This recipe is simple to prepare and can be served as either a starter or a main course.

8 lamb's kidneys (cleaned, fat removed and halved)

oil

4 tomatoes (peeled, deseeded and diced)

8 gherkins (cut in half)

1 large bunch basil (shredded)

100ml balsamic vinegar

1 tablespoon olive oil

4 slices smoked bacon

1. Add a little oil to a heavy pan and sear the kidneys (flat side down first).
2. Season and cook for 2 minutes on each side.
3. Remove and keep warm.
4. Add all the other ingredients to the pan and toss for 1 minute.
5. Add the kidneys and remove the pan from the heat.
6. Cook the bacon under a hot grill until crisp. Serve with the kidneys.

Chargrilled spiced lamb chops with ratatouille and feta cheese

Adding spices to lamb chops really brings them into a different league. Ratatouille is delicious served with lamb, pork or indeed beef. The feta in this dish rounds off a great plateful of flavour.

For the lamb chops

1 tablespoon olive oil

1 tablespoon chopped thyme

12 lamb cutlets

1 tablespoon curry powder or
  spice mix (whatever you have)

For the ratatouille and feta cheese

1 tablespoon olive oil

2 shallots (diced)

2 cloves garlic (crushed)

2 punnets cherry tomatoes

1 tablespoon tomato paste

½ glass white wine

1 red pepper (diced)

2 courgettes (diced)

1 aubergine (diced)

1 tablespoon oregano

100g feta cheese (diced)

For the lamb

1. Mix the oil and thyme and coat the lamb cutlets with the mixture.
2. Season with the spices and salt and pepper.
3. Sear on both sides on a hot griddle pan for about 3 minutes on each side.

For the ratatouille

1. Sauté the shallot and garlic in the olive oil for 1 minute. Add the tomatoes and cook for 2–3 minutes.
2. Add the tomato paste and wine. Season and simmer for 2 minutes.
3. Add the pepper to an oiled pan and sauté for 2 minutes.
4. Add the courgettes and aubergine and cook for 2 minutes.
5. Season and add the tomato sauce and oregano.
6. Just before serving, crumble the feta over the ratatouille and mix gently.

Marinated rump of lamb with red pepper chutney and colcannon

As in many other recipes in this book, this dish uses off-cuts rather than prime cuts. Once these cuts are prepared and cooked properly, the end result can often be better than the prime cuts. There is a little more preparation involved, but it is well worth it. For the colcannon, I have used spring onion rather than the traditional kale, but by all means, if kale is in season, use that.

4 lamb rumps, about 200g each

For the marinade
50ml soy sauce

50ml port

2 tablespoons chopped
   rosemary

2 tablespoons honey

2 tablespoons balsamic vinegar

For the red pepper chutney
1 tablespoon olive oil

1 red onion (sliced)

1 clove garlic (sliced)

½ teaspoon ground cumin

1 sprig thyme

1 bay leaf

2 red peppers (roasted,
   peeled, deseeded, and
   roughly chopped)

1 tablespoon caster sugar

For the lamb
1. Mix all the marinade ingredients together and toss with the lamb. Cover and leave in the fridge overnight.
2. Remove the lamb from the marinade and seal the lamb in a hot oiled pan on all sides. Season.
3. Roast in the oven for 8 minutes (15 minutes for well done) at 180˚C.
4. Leave to rest.

For the red pepper chutney
1. Heat the olive oil in a pan.
2. Gently cook the onion, garlic, cumin, thyme and bay leaf for 4–5 minutes, until the onion is soft.
3. Add the red peppers and sugar and cook for a further 2 minutes.
4. Add the red wine and red wine vinegar.
5. Reduce until all the liquid has evaporated.
6. Season.

2 tablespoons red wine

2 tablespoons red wine vinegar

For the colcannon

3 large rooster potatoes

(peeled and cut into chunks)

100g spring onion (chopped)

oil

For the whipped colcannon potatoes

1. Boil the potatoes in salted water until tender. Drain and mash.
2. Sauté the spring onion in a little oil.
3. Mix the potato and onion together, season with salt and pepper and keep warm.

Pot roasted shoulder of lamb with lentils and raisins

You could use shoulder of lamb on the bone, but it will take longer to cook. Lentils and raisins make an unusual accompaniment that really works. This is a great winter dish that can be prepared the night before you want to serve it. Or put the earthenware dish over a very low heat, go out for a good long walk and this will be ready to enjoy on your return.

1 boned out shoulder of lamb
   (ask your butcher to roll and
   tie it)
oil
2 sprigs thyme
1 sprig rosemary
2 cloves garlic (sliced)
1 litre chicken stock
200g lentils
12 baby onions (peeled)
2 large carrots (peeled and
   sliced)
2 large potatoes (peeled and
   diced)
1 small turnip (peeled and
   diced)
130g raisins
1 bunch mint (chopped)

1. Seal the lamb in a hot oiled pan. Place in an earthenware dish.
2. Add the thyme, rosemary, garlic and chicken stock.
3. Cover and cook in a preheated oven at 160°C for 2 hours.
4. Add the lentils, onions, carrots, potatoes, turnip and raisins and cook for a further 1 hour, until the meat is tender.
5. Sprinkle with chopped fresh mint.

Chicken escalopes with an herb and Parmesan crumb and anchovy and lemon dressing

This is a lovely quick way to cook chicken, and the Parmesan adds an intense flavour. Ideally, use fresh anchovies, but tinned will do. If you do use tinned anchovies, use half the quantity or the flavour will be too strong. The fried egg is an optional extra.

4 chicken breasts (skinned and flattened)
vegetable oil
4 eggs (for frying)

For the crumb
1 egg (beaten)
50ml milk
100g breadcrumbs
1 cup grated Parmesan
1 tablespoon chopped parsley
120g white flour

For the anchovy and lemon dressing
100g anchovies
2 lemons (peeled and cut into segments)
2 tablespoons chopped chives

For the crumb
1. Mix the egg and milk together in a shallow bowl.
2. In a separate shallow bowl, mix the breadcrumbs, Parmesan and parsley.
3. Season the chicken breast and lightly coat in the flour.
4. Dip the chicken into the egg mixture, then coat with the crumb mixture.

To cook the chicken
1. Heat some vegetable oil in a frying pan and cook the chicken on both sides until golden brown (4–5 minutes on each side).

For the anchovy and lemon dressing
1. Mix the anchovies, lemon segments and chives.

To serve
1. Spoon the dressing over the chicken.
2. Fry the eggs and place a fried egg on each chicken breast.
3. Grate over some fresh Parmesan.

Roast glazed leg of lamb
with minestrone

This is a slightly different take on roast leg of lamb. The dark glazed outer surface of the lamb contrasts with the pink flesh inside. Basting throughout the cooking time keeps the meat lovely and moist. Be sure to rest the meat before carving.

1 leg of lamb

1 onion (sliced)

2 carrots (peeled and diced)

1 stick celery (diced)

3 cloves garlic (crushed)

1 sprig thyme

1 sprig rosemary

200ml meat stock (or gravy granules)

100ml red wine

For the minestrone

2 tablespoons olive oil

1 onion (chopped)

2 carrots (diced)

2 sticks celery (diced)

2 cloves garlic (crushed)

400g tin chopped tomatoes

750ml chicken stock (made with a stock cube is fine)

400g cannellini beans or haricot beans (tinned or dried), soaked overnight if dried

2 courgettes (diced)

2 tablespoons chopped parsley

1. On a large, very hot oiled pan, seal the leg of lamb on all sides to a golden brown. Place in a roasting dish.
2. Add the onion, carrot, celery, garlic, thyme and rosemary to the pan in which you sealed the lamb.
3. Toss these in the pan for a couple of minutes.
4. Add the stock (or gravy granules) and the wine.
5. Pour the contents of the pan into the roasting tray around the lamb, but not over it.
6. Place in a moderate oven, 180–185°C.
7. Baste the lamb with the juices from the roasting tray every 15 minutes for the first hour of cooking.
8. After 1 hour, turn the lamb and continue to cook for a further 30 minutes (basting throughout).
9. Remove from the oven and allow to rest on a chopping board for 15 minutes.
10. When carving, always carve from the top, in the direction of the shin.

For the minestrone

1. In a large saucepan, sauté the onion in the olive oil for 1 minute. Add the carrot, celery and garlic.
2. Cook for a further 2 minutes, stirring continuously.
3. Add the tomatoes and stock and season.
4. Simmer over a low heat for 30 minutes.
5. Add the beans and courgette and cook for a further 5 minutes. Add the parsley.

Rack of pork with roast vegetables and apple and cinnamon sauce

The meat will be more moist and flavoursome when cooked on the bone. You could cook the roast vegetables in the same roasting tray as the pork so that they absorb each others' flavours.

1 rack of pork (8 bone)
1 tablespoon chopped rosemary
1 tablespoon chopped thyme
1 tablespoon olive oil
4 bay leaves

For the vegetables

4 large carrots (peeled and
    sliced lengthways)
1 onion (thickly sliced)
½ head celeriac (peeled and
    chopped)
8 baby onions (peeled)
1 parsnip (peeled and sliced)
1 small turnip (peeled and diced)
olive oil
100ml chicken or vegetable stock
2 tablespoons chopped thyme
50ml honey
juice of 2 lemons
2 tablespoons brown sugar
2 tablespoons red wine vinegar

For the apple sauce

2 Granny Smith apples (peeled,
    cored and diced)
1 stick cinnamon
1 star anise
250ml apple juice

For the pork

1. Seal the rack of pork on both sides on a roasting tray over a high heat.
2. Roast in the oven at 180°C for 45–60 minutes, until the juices run clear.
3. Leave to rest for 10 minutes.

For the honey and lemon roast vegetables

1. Blanch all the vegetables in boiling water for 3 minutes.
2. Refresh with cold water.
3. Heat some olive oil in a large pan, then add the vegetables and toss for 2 minutes.
4. Add the chicken stock, thyme, honey, lemon juice, sugar and vinegar and season.
5. Cook over a medium heat until the liquid has almost evaporated.
6. The vegetables should be tender and glazed.

For the apple and cinnamon sauce

1. Put the apple, cinnamon, star anise and apple juice in a saucepan and reduce until the apple is tender.
2. Remove the cinnamon and star anise.
3. Blitz into a purée.

Glazed pork belly with poached apricots and apple and Calvados sauce

The secret here is to remove all the sinews and fat from the pork (your butcher will be happy to do this for you). You can make this dish with any stoned fruits. Apple is, of course, a classic with pork, and the Calvados adds the extra wow.

1 orange (chopped)

1 tablespoon sea salt

1 tablespoon chopped thyme

2 tablespoons five spice powder

1 tablespoon cloves

1 tablespoon cinnamon

800g piece pork belly (excess
  fat and bones removed)

500ml duck fat

For the black pepper glaze

150ml soy sauce

3 tablespoons honey

1 tablespoon cracked black
  pepper

To cook the pork

1. Mix together the orange, salt, thyme, five spice, cloves and cinnamon.
2. Spread the mixture over the pork.
3. Cover and place in the fridge overnight.
4. Remove the pork and wash off the marinade. Pat dry with paper towels.
5. Melt the duck fat and pour over the pork.
6. Roast the meat in a preheated oven for 2½ hours at 150–160˚C.
7. Leave the pork to cool in the fat.
8. When the pork has cooled, place it between two baking trays with a heavy weight on top. Leave overnight.
9. Cut the pork into portions and brown on a hot pan, skin side down first, until golden.
10. Coat with the black pepper glaze.

For the black pepper glaze

1. In a hot saucepan over a low heat, slowly reduce the soy sauce and honey until the mixture reaches a syrupy consistency.
2. Remove from the heat and add the pepper.

For the poached apricots

200ml water

65g sugar

1 teaspoon cinnamon

1 teaspoon cloves

2 apricots (halved and stones removed)

For the apple and Calvados sauce

2 eating apples (peeled, cored and diced)

1 shallot (diced)

a little butter

100ml Calvados

75ml cream

75ml beef or chicken stock (a stock cube is fine)

For the poached apricots

1. Bring the water, sugar, cinnamon and cloves to the boil.
2. Simmer briefly and add the apricots.
3. Remove from the heat.

For the apple and Calvados sauce

1. Sweat the apple and shallot in a little butter.
2. Add the Calvados and flame with a match to burn off the alcohol.
3. Add the cream and stock and reduce to the desired thickness.
4. Season.

Toulouse sausages with Puy lentil cassoulet and tomato chutney

Toulouse sausage – or indeed any gourmet sausage – is perfect in a cassoulet. The cider along with the tomato chutney adds a lovely sweetness to this dish. It's a perfect winter supper.

8 Toulouse sausages (or any gourmet sausage)

2 shallots (diced)

1 carrot (peeled and diced)

1 stick celery (diced)

1 red pepper (diced)

1 clove garlic (crushed)

1 teaspoon tomato paste

2 tomatoes (peeled and chopped)

1 teaspoon thyme

100ml cider

100ml chicken or vegetable stock

100g Puy lentils (blanched)

2 apples (peeled and diced)

For the tomato chutney

1 shallot (diced)

4 tomatoes (peeled and chopped)

1 teaspoon brown sugar

1 teaspoon vinegar

1 teaspoon tomato paste

For the cassoulet

1. Brown the sausages in a frying pan or under the grill.
2. Slowly sweat off the shallot, carrot, celery, pepper and garlic for 5 minutes.
3. Add the tomato paste and chopped tomatoes and thyme and cook for a further 5 minutes.
4. Add the sausages, cider, stock and lentils and simmer for 10–15 minutes.
5. Season and add the apple.

For the tomato and cider chutney

1. Gently sweat the shallot for 5 minutes.
2. Add the tomatoes and cook slowly for 5 minutes.
3. Add the sugar, vinegar and tomato paste.
4. Cook for 10 minutes.
5. Season.

Honey-glazed ham hock with green cabbage

This is an adaptation of the classic Irish dish of bacon and cabbage; it's a great low-cost main course that would satisfy a family of four. Braising the ham slowly makes the meat beautifully tender. Honey and mustard together are fabulous.

4 ham hocks
1 carrot (peeled and chopped)
2 sticks celery (chopped)
1 onion (chopped)
4 bay leaves
1 sprig thyme
1 sprig rosemary
50g English mustard
150ml honey
50g brown sugar
1tbsp cloves
1 large head green cabbage
   (shredded)
2tbsp grain mustard
100ml cream

1. Soak the ham hocks overnight in water to remove excess salt.
2. Strain, cover with water and bring to the boil.
3. Strain again and add enough fresh water to cover the hocks.
4. Add the carrot, celery, onion, bay leaves, thyme and rosemary and simmer very gently for 1½ hours.
5. To check whether the ham hock is cooked, look for the little bone at the end of the hock: if you can remove this bone easily, the hock is cooked.
6. Remove the ham from the cooking broth, strain the broth and retain.
7. Remove the outer skin from the ham.
8. Brush with the mustard, honey and sugar and stud with cloves.
9. Bake in a preheated oven at 160°C for 10 minutes, until golden (baste once or twice while cooking).
10. Using some of the cooking broth, boil the cabbage until tender.
11. In a small pot, simmer a little of the cooking liquid with the grain mustard and cream. Season lightly and serve with the ham hock and cabbage.

Roast cutlet of veal
with gremolata

Veal is available from specialist butchers. It is expensive, so keep this recipe for a special occasion dinner party. I would recommend that the veal is cooked pink to retain as much of the flavour as possible. Gremolata is a classic accompaniment to serve with veal.

4 veal cutlets, about 250g each
oil

For the gremolata
100g Parmesan cheese (grated)
1 clove garlic (finely chopped)
1 tablespoon olive oil
zest and juice of 1 lemon
1 tablespoon parsley (chopped)

1. Season the cutlets, then sear them in a hot oiled pan on both sides until brown.
2. Transfer to the oven and cook for a further 12–15 minutes at 180°C.

For the gremolata
1. Mix all the ingredients together and season with salt and pepper.

Marinated beef skirt with Parma ham and mozzarella

Skirt is one of the cheapest cuts of beef. The secret is to marinate the beef and cook it pink. It's a lovely, tender piece of steak full of flavour. Warm beef always works well in a salad.

For the beef skirt

4 x 150g portions beef skirt

1 teaspoon chopped thyme

1 clove garlic (chopped)

1 teaspoon olive oil

1 teaspoon sea salt

For the tomato sauce

1 onion (chopped)

1 clove garlic (chopped)

olive oil

1 tomato (chopped)

1 tablespoon tomato paste

For the mustard dressing

1 tablespoon olive oil

1 teaspoon Dijon mustard

1 teaspoon honey

juice of ½ lemon

For the bread

1 baguette (sliced)

olive oil

2 tablespoons chopped thyme

4 garlic cloves (crushed)

1 pack sliced Parma ham

250g aged mozzarella cheese

4 oven-dried tomatoes

1 tablespoon black olives

mixed tossed leaves

For the beef skirt

1. Mix together the thyme, garlic, oil and salt.
2. Rub the mixture over the beef and marinate for 2 days in a covered bowl in the fridge.
3. Sauté on a hot pan for 2 minutes on each side.

For the tomato sauce

1. Sweat the onion and garlic in olive oil.
2. Add the tomato and tomato paste, season and simmer slowly for 30 minutes.
3. Allow to cool.

For the mustard dressing

1. Mix all the dressing ingredients in a large bowl.

For the bread

1. Drizzle the olive oil, chopped thyme and garlic over the sliced bread.
2. Bake in the oven at 180˚C until crisp (but not too crisp).
3. Spread the cooled tomato sauce on the bread. Add the cheese, Parma ham, tomato and olives.
4. Bake in the oven at 180°C until golden.

To serve

Slice the beef, place on top of the bread with some salad leaves and drizzle with the mustard dressing.

Rib eye of beef with carrot and cumin purée and Bourguignonne sauce

I much prefer rib eye to fillet. The texture and flavour are far superior, in my opinion: the rib has a nice bite to it, while a fillet can be a little too tender. The carrot and cumin in this dish works brilliantly, as does a carrot and cumin combination in a soup. Bourguignonne sauce is a classic served with beef.

4 rib eye steaks

For the Bourguignonne sauce

olive oil
100g pearl (pickling) onions
(peeled and blanched)
100g streaky bacon
100g wild mushrooms
(or cultivated)
½ glass red wine
200ml demi-glaze or gravy

For the carrot and cumin purée

5 carrots (peeled and roughly chopped)
1 shallot (halved)
1 clove garlic (crushed)
1 teaspoon ground cumin (optional)
1 tablespoon water
2 tablespoons olive oil
salt and freshly ground white pepper

For the beef

1. Season the beef with black pepper and sea salt.
2. Sear the beef on a hot pan.
3. Cook on both sides for 5 minutes for rare/medium. Continue to cook for a further few minutes for well done.

For the Bourguignonne sauce

1. Heat the oil in a pan. Sauté the onions and bacon and add the mushrooms.
2. Add the red wine and demi-glaze or gravy.
3. Reduce until the sauce reaches the desired consistency.

For the carrot and cumin purée

1. Preheat the oven to 180°C.
2. Place the carrots, shallot, garlic, cumin and water in a roasting tin and stir in the olive oil.
3. Cover with tinfoil and roast for 35–40 minutes, until tender.
4. Pulverise the carrot mixture in a food processor until smooth.
5. Season with salt and white pepper.

Roast rib of beef with Yorkshire pudding stuffed with red onion relish and horseradish cream

This is my all-time favourite meat to cook for a dinner party, as you can be absolutely sure it will be a real party pleaser. Red onion and horseradish is absolutely delicious. If you are cooking for ten or more, I would recommend a larger piece of meat, cooked with the bone in.

2kg piece rib eye of beef
  (off the bone)

For the red onion relish
60g butter
2 red onions (finely sliced)
2 tablespoons brown sugar
1 bay leaf
4 cloves
pinch of cinnamon
2 tablespoons red wine vinegar
1 sprig thyme

For the horseradish cream
100g freshly grated horseradish
  (or 2 tablespoons
  prepared horseradish)
150ml whipped cream
1 tablespoon chopped chives

For the beef
1. Preheat the oven to 190°C.
2. Season the beef with black pepper and sea salt.
3. Seal the beef on all sides on a hot oiled pan.
4. Transfer to the oven and roast for 50 minutes (rare) or 1½ hours (well done).
5. Allow to rest before carving.

For the red onion relish
1. In a heavy-based saucepan, melt the butter and add the red onions.
2. Season, toss and cook for 5 minutes.
3. Add the sugar, bay leaf, thyme, cloves and cinnamon. Cook for a further 5 minutes, then and add the red wine vinegar and thyme.
4. Cover the pan and simmer very slowly for 45 minutes. Allow to cool.

For the horseradish cream
1. Mix the horseradish and cream together. Add the chives.

For the Yorkshire pudding

130g flour

1 teaspoon salt

2 large eggs

200ml whole milk

4 tablespoons vegetable oil
   or beef fat

For the Yorkshire pudding

1. In a blender, blend the flour, salt, eggs and milk until just smooth.
2. Cover the batter and chill for 30 minutes.
3. Preheat the oven to 200°C.
4. Take a large cupcake tray and pour the oil into each cup.
5. Put the tray in the middle of the oven for 5 minutes to heat the oil (it must be hot).
6. Quickly pour half a cup of batter into each cup and bake in the middle of the oven until the puddings are puffed and golden brown, about 18 minutes.
7. Using tongs, remove the puddings from the tray.
8. Add the red onion relish, top with a dollop of horseradish cream and serve immediately with the beef.

Casserole of oxtail with baby leeks and sweet potato purée

Oxtail is very rarely used, although it is packed with flavour. Instead of serving this as a main course, you could serve it as a garnish with a small steak. Once the oxtail is cooked, chill it, remove the meat and then reshape the meat. Sweet potato purée is simple and full of delicious flavour.

vegetable oil
4 oxtails (cut into large pieces)
1 onion (diced)
2 cloves garlic (crushed)
1 carrot (peeled and chopped)
1 stick celery (chopped)
1 tablespoon tomato paste
300ml beef stock
200ml red wine
1 tablespoon chopped thyme
2 tablespoons Worcestershire sauce
4 tomatoes (chopped)
8 baby leeks (cleaned)

For the sweet potato purée

4 sweet potatoes
2 tablespoons olive oil

For the casserole

1. In a heavy-based saucepan, heat a little vegetable oil and seal the oxtails on all sides.
2. Season and add the onion, garlic, carrot and celery.
3. Sauté for 5 minutes.
4. Add the tomato paste, stock, wine, thyme and Worcestershire sauce.
5. Cover the pot and slowly braise for 2–3 hours, until tender.
6. Remove the oxtails and strain the liquid into a saucepan.
7. Add the tomatoes and leeks to the liquid and cook for 10 minutes, until tender.

For the sweet potato purée

1. Bake the sweet potatoes in their skins in the oven at 150˚C for 1 hour.
2. When they are tender, scrape out the flesh and purée with olive oil. Season.

Slow-cooked short rib of beef chasseur

Short rib of beef is classified as an off-cut, but if you cook it slowly you get beautifully gelatinous, tender meat. The slower and lower you cook this cut of meat, the better the results. Chasseur sauce makes a great accompaniment not only to beef, but also to chicken.

1 tablespoon vegetable oil
8 short ribs of beef
1 onion (diced)
1 stick celery (diced)
1 carrot (peeled and diced)
2 cloves garlic (diced)
1 small leek (diced)
2 bay leaves
1 tablespoon tarragon
450ml beef stock
100ml red wine
150ml balsamic vinegar

For the chasseur sauce

50g butter
2 shallots (diced)
250g button mushrooms
4 tomatoes (peeled and diced)
4 tablespoons gherkins (sliced)
2 tablespoons tarragon

For the beef

1. Heat the oil in a pan. Seal the ribs on both sides in the hot oil and season. Transfer to a roasting dish.
2. Put the onion, celery, carrot, garlic, leek, bay leaves and tarragon in the pan in which you seared the beef.
3. Sweat for 4–5 minutes over a moderate heat.
4. Add the stock, red wine and balsamic vinegar.
5. Simmer for 10 minutes.
6. Add to the roasting tin.
7. Roast in a preheated oven at 160˚C for about 4 hours (or until tender).
8. Remove the ribs and strain the liquid into a saucepan.
9. Over a low heat, reduce the sauce by half or until it reaches the desired consistency. Set aside.

For the chasseur sauce

1. Melt the butter in a pan.
2. Sweat the shallots for 2 minutes without browning.
3. Add the mushrooms and cook for a further 2–3 minutes.
4. Add the tomatoes, gherkins and tarragon.
5. Check the seasoning.
6. Add this mixture to the sauce set aside earlier.

5

Fish

Poached fillets of lemon sole with tomato and pepper purée and basil aïoli

Poaching lemon sole works very well. Never bring the water above a slow simmer. If you prefer not to make your own aïoli, just add some puréed basil to some mayonnaise. The red, white and green in this dish is truly superb visually.

For the tomato and pepper purée

4 plum tomatoes (halved)
2 red peppers (halved and
    deseeded)
olive oil
1 onion (diced)
1 leek (diced)
2 cloves garlic (crushed)
1 carrot (diced)
butter
1 tablespoon white wine vinegar
1 tablespoon tomato paste
1 tablespoon brown sugar
100ml chicken stock

For the sole

8 x 90g lemon sole fillets
    (skinned and rolled)
2 bay leaves
1 tablespoon white wine vinegar
1 teaspoon sea salt

For the tomato and pepper purée

1. Place the tomatoes and peppers in a roasting tray.
2. Drizzle with olive oil and roast in the oven for 25 minutes at 180°C.
3. Remove the skins from the peppers.
4. In a heavy pot, sweat the onion, leek, garlic and carrot in a little butter for 5 minutes.
5. Add the tomatoes and peppers with the vinegar, tomato paste, sugar and stock.
6. Simmer for 30 minutes over a low heat.
7. Liquidise and pass through a sieve.

For the sole

1. Poach the fillets of sole in gently simmering water with the bay leaves, vinegar and salt for 5–7 minutes.
2. Ensure the fish is covered with the liquid.

For the basil aïoli

4 garlic cloves (crushed)

2 egg yolks

handful fresh basil leaves

250ml olive oil

1 tablespoon fresh lemon juice

For the basil aïoli

1. Place the garlic, egg yolks and basil in a blender.
2. Blend for 1 minute, then slowly drizzle in the olive oil.
3. Continue to slowly add the olive oil until the mixture reaches the consistency of mayonnaise.
4. Season to taste, then add the lemon juice.
5. Transfer to a plastic bottle and chill until needed.

Plaice on the bone with chillies, garlic and ginger

Plaice on the bone is one of my favourite fish. It's very important to use the freshest of fresh plaice. A classic combination of chilli, garlic and ginger is great with this, but the plaice could also be served plain with melted herb butter.

vegetable oil

4 large plaice on the bone (trimmed and cleaned)

4 red chillies (deseeded and diced)

4 cloves garlic (sliced)

1 large piece of fresh ginger (peeled and sliced)

1 tablespoon olive oil

2 tablespoons sherry vinegar

1 tablespoon sesame oil

2 tablespoons chopped curly parsley

2 lemons

1. Set 2 large non-stick frying pans on a high heat and add a little vegetable oil.
2. Cook the fish on both sides for about 2–3 minutes on each side.
3. Season with sea salt and pepper.
4. In a clean pan over a high heat, fry the chillies, garlic and ginger in the olive oil for 10 seconds.
5. Remove the pan from the heat and add the vinegar, sesame oil and parsley.
6. Spoon the sauce over the fish and dress with the lemons.

Seared Dover sole with hazelnut dressing

Dover sole/black sole is very expensive, so this dish is best saved for a special occasion. Believe it or not, sole is one of the very few fish that is better if left for two or three days after it is caught before cooking: this allows the fish to mature. A nutty dressing is a classic accompaniment to sole.

For the Dover sole

4 tablespoons vegetable oil
50g butter
4 Dover sole, about 350–400g
150g sieved flour

For the hazelnut dressing

1 tablespoon white wine vinegar
pinch of caster sugar
pinch of salt
4 tablespoons extra virgin
   olive oil
½ teaspoon Dijon mustard
3 tablespoon chopped, roasted
   and skinned hazelnuts

For the Dover sole

1. Heat a large pan over a high heat. (If you do not have a pan big enough to take all the fish at once, you can cook it in batches.)
2. Add the oil and the butter, taking care not to burn the butter.
3. Toss the sole in the flour (coating both sides) and place on the pan.
4. Turn the heat down to medium and cook for 4–5 minutes, turning the fish when it is golden brown.
5. Cook for a further 3–5 minutes on the other side and remove from the pan.

For the hazelnut dressing

1. Place the vinegar in a screw-topped jar. Add the sugar and a good pinch of salt and shake the jar until the salt has dissolved.
2. Add the oil to the jar with the mustard and shake again until a thick emulsion forms.
3. Season to taste and stir in the hazelnuts.
4. Chill until required.

Poached ray wing, bacon and barley broth

Ray wing is very popular in Dublin, and all the chippers have ray on Fridays. But this recipe is a lot healthier than the way the chippers cook ray. It's poached with an Irish slant, using bacon and barley. You could cook this on the bone, but it is better to ask your fishmonger to bone the fish for you. It can be tricky to do this yourself, but if you want to try it, just follow the line of the bones with a very sharp knife.

200g cured bacon (diced)

100g barley

4 bay leaves

50g baby onions (peeled)

½ head of celery

2 large carrots (peeled and cut into large chunks)

1 fennel bulb (cut in lengths)

4 x 120g pieces of ray wing (boned)

1 bunch fresh parsley (chopped)

1. In a large pot, bring the bacon to the boil in water.
2. Strain off the water and add 1 litre of fresh water.
3. Bring to a simmer, add the barley and bay leaves, and simmer gently for 20 minutes.
4. Add the onions, celery, carrot and fennel and simmer until the vegetables are tender.
5. Add the ray wing, simmer for 5–7 minutes and add the parsley.

Baked cod fillet with herb crumble and mussel and tomato vinaigrette

The flavour and texture of cod are absolutely perfect. It's a lovely fresh fish, very simply prepared in this recipe. The herbs used in the crumble are soft and flavoursome. The tomato vinaigrette is ideal to serve with mussels.

This dish is very healthy, nutritious and low in calories. One tip is to always undercook fish slightly because it will continue to cook when it is removed from the oven. Overcooking the fish would ruin the dish. The cod would be delicious served with a crisp green salad and some boiled baby potatoes.

olive oil

4 x 180g pieces of cod (skinned)

finely chopped soft herbs
(parsley, chives, chervil)

100g white breadcrumbs

sea salt and white pepper

For the vinaigrette

100ml good-quality extra virgin
olive oil

30ml white wine vinegar

150g mussels from a jar or
cooked fresh mussels

50g roasted pine nuts

24 cherry tomatoes (halved
and oven dried with chopped
herbs and some garlic for
2 hours at 60°C)

lemon wedges (optional)

1. Add a little olive oil to a hot non-stick frying pan.
2. Brown the cod on both sides.
3. In a bowl, combine the chopped herbs with the breadcrumbs, season with sea salt and white pepper and mix well.
4. Press the breadcrumb mixture onto one side of each piece of cod.
5. Bake in a moderate oven at 180°C for 3–4 minutes.

For the vinaigrette

1. In a bowl, combine the olive oil and vinegar.
2. Add the mussels (after straining off the juices), pine nuts and cherry tomato halves.
3. Season to taste.
4. Divide the vinaigrette between four serving plates and place the cod on top.
5. Serve with wedges of lemon if desired.

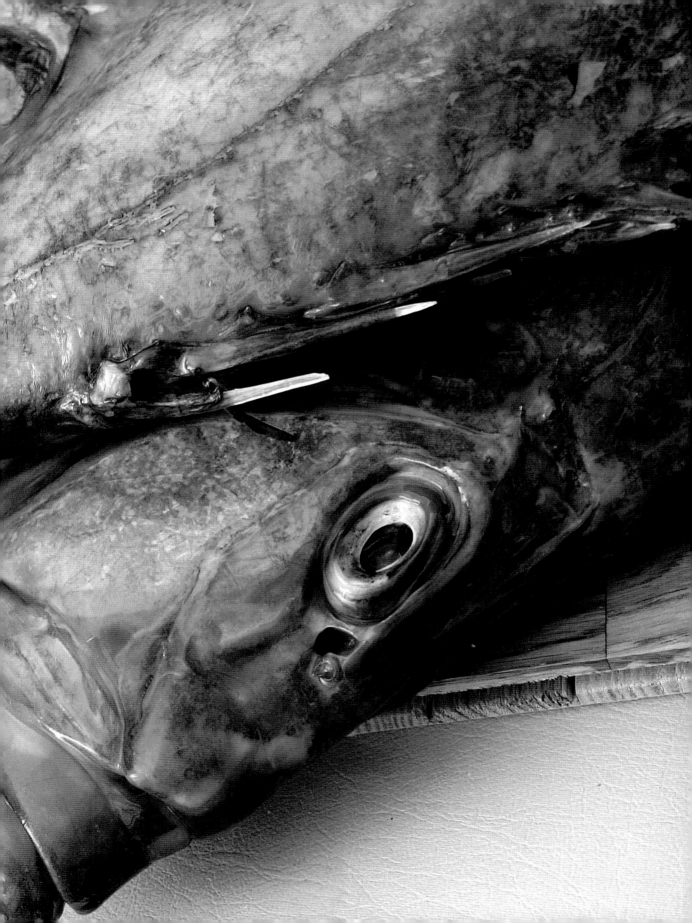

Devilled whitebait with natural yoghurt and cucumber

I often cook this dish – it's an old favourite of mine. One of the reasons I love it is because of its simplicity. Fresh whitebait is best, but frozen will also give you a good result. The cucumber and natural yoghurt adds a lovely freshness to the fish.

For the devilled whitebait

50g sieved flour

50g sweet paprika

400g whitebait, fresh or frozen

vegetable oil, for deep frying

For the yoghurt and cucumber

1 cucumber (quartered, deseeded and diced)

200ml natural yoghurt

1 tablespoon chopped parsley

For the devilled whitebait

1. Mix the flour and paprika together.
2. Toss the whitebait in the flour mixture.
3. Deep fry in hot, clean vegetable oil at 180°C for 3–4 minutes, until crisp.
4. Drain on paper towels and season with salt and freshly ground black pepper.

For the yoghurt and cucumber

1. Combine all the ingredients together in a bowl.

Whole baked brill and carrots with mustard and onion cream

Baking fish on the bone makes such a huge difference to the flavour. If you feel you are up to the challenge, impress your guests at a dinner party by taking the fish off the bone at the table before serving.

For the carrots with mustard and onion cream

2 shallots (diced)

a little butter

400ml fish stock

200ml white wine

200ml cream

16 baby carrots (peeled and blanched)

16 baby onions (peeled and blanched)

2 tablespoons Dijon mustard

2 tablespoons chopped fresh dill

For the brill

1 whole brill (about 2kg)

1 tablespoon olive oil

2 cloves garlic (sliced)

1 tablespoon chopped thyme

1 glass white wine

For the carrots with mustard and onion cream

1. Sweat the shallots in butter in a saucepan for 2 minutes (do not brown).
2. Add the fish stock and cook briskly until reduced by half.
3. Add the wine and reduce by half.
4. Add the cream and reduce for a further 5 minutes.
5. Add the carrots, onions and mustard.
6. Season and add the dill.

For the brill

1. Place the brill on a roasting tray and cover with the oil, garlic, thyme and wine.
2. Season with freshly ground black pepper and sea salt.
3. Bake in the oven for 30–40 minutes at 160˚C.

Spiced monkfish with carrot and orange purée and carrot and ginger salad

When I started cooking, monkfish used to be available free of charge. Now it really is a premium fish. Monkfish has a tendency to be wet, but in this recipe the spices absorb the moisture. There is a lovely contrast between the colourful spiced outside of the fish and the white meat. Shredded carrot and ginger is wonderfully simple and fresh.

4 x 160g monkfish portions
    (trimmed)
1 tablespoon vegetable oil

For the spice mix

1 teaspoon cumin seeds (crushed)
1 teaspoon coriander seeds
    (crushed)
pinch of five spice powder
¼ red chilli (deseeded and diced)
1cm piece of root ginger
    (peeled and finely diced)
1 clove garlic (crushed)

For the carrot and orange purée

2 tablespoons olive oil
2 shallots (diced)
1 clove garlic (crushed)
4 large carrots (peeled and
    chopped)
salt and freshly ground white
    pepper
juice of 2 oranges

For the spiced monkfish

1. Mix all the spice mix ingredients together in a large bowl.
2. Toss the monkfish on all sides in the spice mix.
3. Add the vegetable oil to a hot pan.
4. Brown the fish on all sides.
5. Finish in the oven at 180°C for 3–4 minutes.
6. Remove and rest for a few minutes before serving.

For the carrot and orange purée

1. Add the olive oil to a heavy saucepan and gently cook the shallots and garlic for 2 minutes.
2. Add the carrots, season with salt and freshly ground white pepper and cook for 3 minutes.
3. Add the orange juice.
4. Cook very slowly for 20 minutes, or until the carrots are very tender.
5. Pulverise the mixture in a food processor.

For the carrot and ginger salad

1. Toss the carrots, ginger and chervil in a large bowl.
2. Season and drizzle with olive oil.

For the carrot and ginger salad

2 large carrots (peeled and grated)

5cm piece of root ginger (peeled and grated)

1 tablespoon chopped fresh chervil

1 tablespoon olive oil

To serve

Take four plates, spread a circle of the carrot purée on each, place the fish on top of the purée and some of the carrot and ginger salad on top.

Stuffed fillet of hake with Parma ham and pea and shallot dressing

The great thing about wrapping fish in Parma ham is that it makes each portion look identical, eliminating the 'top and tail' look. I think frozen peas work best in this dish.

For the hake

4 slices Parma ham
600g fillet of hake (skinned)
1 tablespoon chopped parsley
1 clove garlic (crushed)
zest of 1 lemon (retain the juice)

For the pea purée

500g frozen peas
1 clove garlic (crushed)
butter
cream

For the pea and shallot dressing

500g frozen peas
4 shallots (diced)
1 clove garlic (crushed)
1 tablespoon olive oil
1 tablespoon white wine vinegar
1 tablespoon chopped chives

1. Place the slices of Parma ham side by side on a large sheet of clingfilm.
2. Place the hake on top of the ham.
3. Mix the parsley, garlic and lemon zest and spread the mixture along the centre of the fish.
4. Season and roll up tightly, using the clingfilm to pull the roll together.
5. Refrigerate for 2 hours.
6. Remove the clingfilm and cut the fish into slices (not too thin).
7. Sear on a hot pan for 2–3 minutes on each side.

For the pea purée

1. Boil the peas until tender. Drain and add the garlic.
2. Season and add a little butter and cream.
3. Mash until smooth.

For the pea and shallot dressing

1. Defrost the peas.
2. Sweat the shallots and garlic in a little of the olive oil.
3. Remove from the heat and add the peas and the rest of the olive oil.
4. Season and add the vinegar, retained lemon juice and chives.

Seared John Dory with crushed new potatoes and olive tapenade

John Dory is also known as Saint Pierre. The marking on the fish is sometimes referred to as St Peter's thumbprint, which was supposedly left on the fish when he lifted it from the sea. John Dory is slightly expensive, but a definite favourite of mine. It's a great meaty fish. There's nothing better than new season Irish potatoes, simply boiled and crushed, to go with this. The potato and black olive tapenade could be served as a salad rather than as an accompaniment.

For the fish
vegetable oil

4 large John Dory fillets

juice of ½ lemon

For the potatoes
600g new potatoes

150g pitted black olives

4 shallots (diced)

2 tablespoons chopped chives

2 spring onions (chopped)

200ml olive oil

1 tablespoon sherry

For the tapenade
300g pitted black olives

2 tablespoons grated
   Parmesan cheese

2 tablespoons olive oil

For the John Dory
1. Add a little vegetable oil to a non-stick frying pan.
2. Cook the fish, skin side down first, for 3 minutes on each side.
3. Season and add the lemon juice.

For the potatoes
1. Cook the potatoes in lightly salted boiling water until tender.
2. Strain and lightly crush with a fork.
3. Add all the other ingredients and season.

For the tapenade
Liquidise all the ingredients together until smooth.

Seared sea bass with tomato confit and red onion and bacon vinaigrette

Wild sea bass can be difficult to source and quite expensive, so if you can't get hold of wild sea bass, use farmed fish instead. The tomato confit is great served with the sea bass, but it can also be used as a soup garnish or in a sandwich.

For the tomato confit

50g brown sugar

50ml red wine vinegar

400g tin tomatoes

1 bay leaf

For the red onion and bacon vinaigrette

2 shallots (sliced)

200g cured bacon (diced)

a little olive oil

25g brown sugar

1 tablespoon balsamic vinegar

75ml port

1 red onion (diced)

For the sea bass

4 fillets of sea bass (scaled and pinboned)

sunflower oil

salt and cracked white pepper

juice of ½ lemon

For the tomato confit

1. Place all the ingredients in a heavy-based saucepan and cook over a very low heat for 1 hour or until most of the liquid has evaporated.

2. Remove the bay leaf. Season and allow to cool.

For the red onion and bacon vinaigrette

1. Sauté the shallot and bacon in a little olive oil until the bacon is lightly browned.

2. Add the sugar, vinegar and port. Cook briskly until reduced by half.

3. Add the red onion and season.

For the sea bass

1. Trim the sea bass and divide into portions of about 80g each.

2. Heat the frying pan and coat in sunflower oil.

3. Season both sides of the fish with salt and cracked white pepper.

4. Place carefully in the pan, skin side down.

5. When the skin is crisp, turn the fish over and lower the heat if necessary.

6. Cook for a further 2–3 minutes.
7. Pour the lemon juice over the fish and remove from the pan.

To serve

1. Place some of the tomato confit in a bowl. Place the sea bass on top of the confit.
2. Spoon the dressing over the sea bass. Finish with a drizzle of olive oil.
3. Season to taste.

Sardines
with sweet peppers

Ask your fishmonger to remove the sardines' backbones. This is a perfect light lunch, which can be served hot or cold with some crusty bread.

For the sardines

2 red chillies (deseeded and
    finely chopped)
1 tablespoon olive oil
1 tablespoon soy sauce
12 fresh sardines (cleaned and
    gutted, backbones removed)
2 tablespoons chopped coriander
zest of 1 lime

For the peppers

4 red peppers (deseeded and
    cut into quarters)
2 tablespoons honey
1 tablespoon olive oil
juice of 2 limes (use the juice
    of the zested lime above for
    half of this)
1 red onion (thinly sliced)

For the sardines

1. Mix the chillies, olive oil and soy sauce.
2. Press down on the back of each fish so that they stand upright.
3. Place the fish on a baking tray.
4. Brush the chilli mixture over the fish and season with salt and pepper.
5. Bake in a hot oven for 5 minutes at 190°C.
6. Remove from the oven and sprinkle with the coriander and lime zest.

For the peppers

1. Brush the pepper quarters with a little oil.
2. Place under a grill or bake in a hot oven until the skin blackens.
3. Remove and allow to cool.
4. In a saucepan, gently simmer the honey, olive oil and lime juice for 5 minutes.
5. Season, add the red onion and allow to cool.
6. Add the red peppers.

Seared sea bream with squid and chorizo orzo and garlic mayonnaise

Even on its own, this orzo is a meal in itself. Make a real dish of it by serving with sea bream, which is a tasty and reasonably priced fish.

For the squid and chorizo orzo

200g orzo pasta
1 shallot (diced)
1 clove garlic (crushed)
1 carrot (peeled and diced)
100g chorizo (diced)
juice of 1 lemon
2 tablespoons white wine
4 squid (cleaned and sliced)
2 tablespoons chopped chives

For the garlic mayonnaise

1 clove garlic (crushed)
200ml mayonnaise
1 teaspoon chopped chives

For the sea bream

4 sea bream (gutted and filleted)
olive oil

For the orzo

1. Cook the orzo in boiling salted water for 10 minutes.
2. Drain and set aside in a heavy-based saucepan.
3. Sauté the shallot, garlic, carrot and chorizo for 3 minutes. Add the lemon juice and wine.
4. In a separate hot oiled pan, sauté the squid quickly for 1 minute.
5. Add the squid to the chorizo mixture with the orzo and chives.
6. Season.

For the mayonnaise

1. Mix all the ingredients together.

For the sea bream

1. Sear the fillets with a little olive oil on a hot pan (skin side down first) for 2 minutes on each side.
2. Season.

Grilled haddock, white beans and chorizo with tomato and pepper

Haddock is a reasonably priced fish, but it is quite underused. This is a great dish for the health conscious, and the beans and tomato complement each other really well. The spring onion salad is a perfect light accompaniment to this fish.

For the white beans and chorizo

6 plum tomatoes (skinned and deseeded)

4 red peppers (deseeded and halved)

2 tablespoons olive oil

1 onion (diced)

1 clove garlic (crushed)

1 chilli (deseeded and diced)

1 carrot (peeled and diced)

1 stick celery (diced)

1 tablespoon tomato paste

4 tablespoons diced chorizo

4 tablespoons cooked white beans

For the haddock

4 x 180g haddock fillets

For the salad

8 spring onions

1 tablespoon olive oil

juice of 1 lemon

1 tablespoon white wine vinegar

1. Preheat the oven to 180°C.
2. Place the tomatoes and peppers in a roasting tray, drizzle with some of the olive oil and roast for 25 minutes.
3. Allow to cool and remove the skins.
4. Heat the rest of the olive oil in a large saucepan.
5. Cook the onion, garlic and chilli until soft.
6. Add the peppers, tomato, carrot and celery.
7. Cook gently for 3 minutes. Add the tomato paste and simmer for 30 minutes.
8. Liquidise and season to taste.
9. Toss the chorizo in a little oil and fry until brown.
10. Add the chorizo and beans to the pepper and tomato mixture.

For the haddock

1. Brush the fish with a little butter or olive oil, season with salt and pepper, and a little lemon juice if you like, place on a tray and grill under a medium heat for about 3 minutes on each side.

For the salad

1. Clean and chop the spring onions.
2. Toss with the olive oil, lemon juice, vinegar and seasoning.

Crisp battered smoked haddock with pickled cucumber and coriander and lime mayonnaise

Smoked haddock and cucumber really complement each other. In this recipe, I have battered the haddock, but for a healthier option you could grill it and serve with the same garnish.

For the batter
80ml iced water
100g cornflour

For the haddock
8 x 75g pieces of smoked haddock (skinned, naturally smoked if possible)
seasoned flour
vegetable oil, for deep frying

For the coriander and lime mayonnaise
200ml mayonnaise
2 tablespoons chopped coriander
zest and juice of 1 lime

For the pickled cucumber
100ml white wine vinegar
150g sugar
1 tablespoon fennel seeds
1 cucumber (deseeded and diced)

For the batter
1. Add the water to the cornflour in a bowl.
2. Beat until it reaches a batter consistency.

For the haddock
1. Toss the smoked haddock in seasoned flour and shake off the excess.
2. Dip in the batter and deep fry in vegetable oil until golden brown.

For the coriander and lime mayonnaise
1. Mix all the ingredients together and season.

For the pickled cucumber
1. Boil the vinegar, sugar, fennel seeds and seasoning for 3–4 minutes.
2. Allow to cool and add the cucumber.

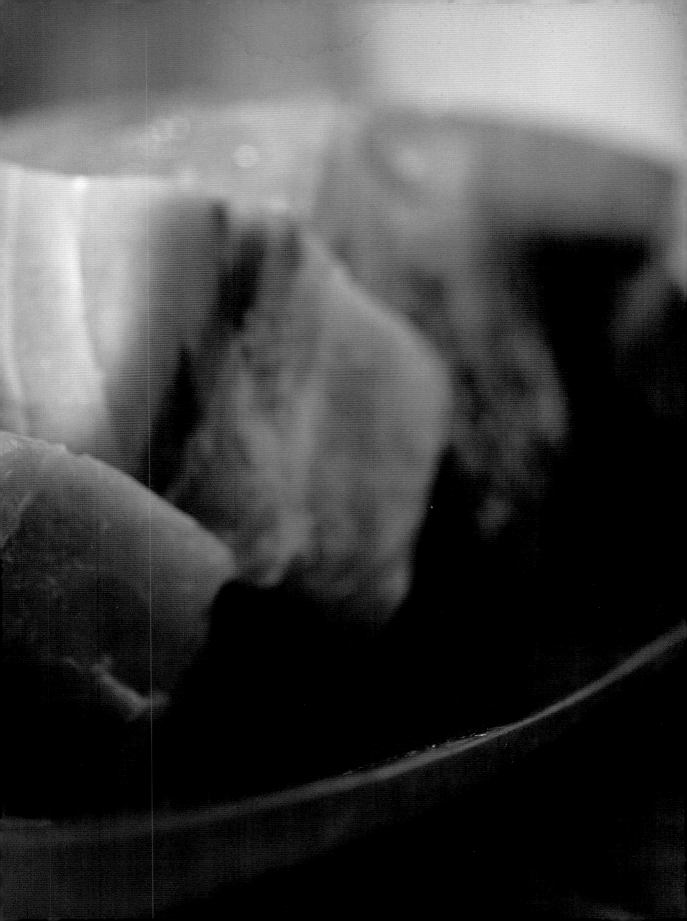

Smoked haddock and crab cakes with English mustard cream and crispy crab toes

When buying smoked haddock, try to source naturally smoked rather than dyed fish, as the difference in flavour is unbelievable. Fish that is naturally smoked looks white, whereas dyed fish looks yellow or orange. You could use cod, whiting or salmon instead of the haddock. The crab toes are optional.

For the fishcakes

250g smoked haddock (preferably naturally smoked), finely chopped or cooked in a little milk and flaked

150g white crab meat

1 tablespoon Thai fish sauce

1 tablespoon chopped dill

1 tablespoon chopped parsley

200g mashed potatoes

1 red chilli (deseeded and chopped)

sunflower or vegetable oil

For the breadcrumbs

1 egg, beaten

50ml milk

120g seasoned flour

100g fresh white breadcrumbs

For the fishcakes

1. Mix all the ingredients together and season.
2. Shape into round cakes about 8cm across.

For the breadcrumbs

1. Beat the egg and milk together.
2. Dip each fish cake into the flour, then into the egg, then into the breadcrumbs.
3. Shallow fry in sunflower or vegetable oil until golden on both sides.
4. Finish in the oven for 10 minutes at 180˚C.

For the crab toes

1. Add the sesame oil to a hot wok or frying pan.
2. Toss the crab toes for 30 seconds.
3. Add the chilli, garlic, ginger and onion.
4. Toss for a further 30 seconds.
5. Add the dill and soy sauce.
6. Season.

For the crab toes

sesame oil

200g crab toes

1 red chilli (deseeded and
  chopped)

2 cloves garlic (sliced)

100g ginger (peeled and sliced)

½ red onion (diced)

1 tablespoon chopped fresh dill

2 tablespoons soy sauce

For the mustard cream

2 tablespoons English mustard

150ml mayonnaise

50ml cream

For the mustard cream

1. Mix all the ingredients together and refrigerate until
    ready to use.

Roast halibut with beetroot, bacon and black pudding dressing and horseradish cream

Try to use wild halibut if possible, although this can be difficult to source. Farmed halibut is easier to find. The freshness of the fish with the earthy taste of the beetroot is a superb combination. Instead of using horseradish cream, you could try grating fresh horseradish over the fish.

For the dressing

200ml red wine
1 tablespoon brown sugar
30ml Cabernet vinegar
30ml olive oil
100g cured dried bacon (diced)
100g black pudding (diced)
1 beetroot (cooked and diced)

For the halibut

4 halibut fillets
a little oil
a little lemon juice

For the horseradish cream

1 tablespoon horseradish sauce
2 tablespoons crème fraîche

For the dressing

1. Reduce the red wine and sugar by half over a low heat until the liquid reaches a sauce-like consistency.
2. Add the vinegar and reduce again.
3. Heat the oil in a pan. Fry the bacon and pudding in a hot oiled pan until lightly browned.
4. Add to the sauce with the beetroot. Season to taste and keep warm.

For the roast halibut

1. In a hot oiled pan, sear the halibut on both sides for 2 minutes on each side. Season with salt, pepper and lemon juice.
2. Finish in the oven for 5 minutes at 180°C.

For the horseradish cream

1. Mix together the horseradish and crème fraîche and stir until creamy.

Steamed salmon fillet with fennel and dill

Steaming salmon keeps the flavour to a maximum. It also retains all the lovely aromas from the dill and fennel. Wild salmon is no longer available in Ireland. We use Clare Island salmon, which is the next best thing. I note that a lot of our guests in the restaurant are requesting steamed vegetables lately. Bamboo steamers are an inexpensive must-have for all home kitchens.

1 tbsp olive oil

1 tsp honey

1 tsp soy sauce

4 x 160g salmon fillets
(skinned)

2 fennel bulbs

1 large bunch dill (chopped)

1. Mix the oil, honey and soy sauce.
2. Coat the salmon fillets with the honey mixture.
3. Season with sea salt and freshly ground black pepper.
4. Cut the fennel lengthways and place in a bamboo steamer.
5. Add the salmon, cover and steam for 5–7 minutes.
6. Add the chopped dill.
7. Steam for a further minute and serve.

Chargrilled swordfish steak with tomato dressing and avocado and lime

Chargrilling fish is a healthy way of cooking it, and the marks from the grill give the fish good visual appeal for presentation. This is a very popular dish during the barbecue season. You could use tuna or salmon instead of swordfish.

For the swordfish

2 red chillies (deseeded and chopped)
1 tablespoon olive oil
1 tablespoon chopped thyme
4 x 160g swordfish steaks

For the tomato dressing

2 tomatoes (peeled, deseeded and diced)
1 tablespoon chopped coriander
1 tablespoon rice wine or Chardonnay
1 tablespoon olive oil
a few drops Tabasco sauce

For the avocado and lime

2 avocados (peeled and finely diced)
juice of 1 lime
1 tablespoon coriander

For the swordfish

1. Mix the chillies, oil and thyme and rub onto the swordfish steaks.
2. Season.
3. Heat a grill or barbecue until very hot.
4. Sear the fish (allowing it to become marked) on both sides, about 3–4 minutes for each side.

For the tomato dressing

1. Combine all the ingredients in a bowl and season.

For the avocado and lime

1. Liquidise all the ingredients in a blender. Season.

Bluefin tuna au poivre with stir-fried greens and béarnaise sauce

You could also use yellowfin tuna, swordfish or salmon for this dish. Tuna is always very popular on our menus in the restaurant. The richness of the béarnaise sauce really works well with the rice wine-sweetened stir-fry. For a healthier option, serve this dish without the béarnaise sauce.

For the tuna

4 x 160g fresh bluefin tuna fillets
2 tablespoons cracked black pepper
1 tablespoon chopped thyme

For the stir-fried greens

2 tablespoons sunflower oil
150g green beans (topped and tailed)
150g sugar snap peas or garden peas
1 head pak choi (chopped)
1 bunch broccoli (blanched)
2 tablespoons soy sauce
1 tablespoon rice wine

For the béarnaise sauce

50ml white wine vinegar
1 sprig thyme
1 bay leaf
1 shallot (diced)
4 egg yolks
250g butter
2 tablespoons chopped tarragon
juice of 1 lemon

For the tuna

1. Toss the tuna in the black pepper and thyme.
2. Sear on a hot pan for 2 minutes on each side.

For the stir-fried greens

1. Heat the oil in a wok and add the vegetables.
2. Stir-fry for 2–3 minutes, making sure the vegetables stay crunchy.
3. Season with salt and pepper.
4. Add the soy sauce and the rice wine.

For the béarnaise sauce

1. Simmer the vinegar, thyme, bay leaf and shallot in a pan until reduced by half.
2. Strain, retaining the liquid.
3. Whisk the egg yolks very slowly into the vinegar mixture over a low heat.
4. Add the butter, whisking continuously.
5. If the sauce curdles, you can save it by whisking in a tablespoon of cold water.
6. Season and add the tarragon and lemon juice.

Seared scallops with black pudding, fennel, apple and candied fruit

The first chef who tried this combination of scallops and black pudding was the late Michael Clifford, and what a great combination it is. The fresh taste of the sea from the scallops combined with the richness of the black pudding is superb.

8 large scallops (roe removed, cleaned and cut in half)

4 large slices black pudding

2 heads fennel (outer skin removed and sliced very finely)

2 green apples (cored and diced)

50ml olive oil

50ml Chardonnay vinegar

1 tablespoon fennel seeds

1 teaspoon vanilla seeds from a pod

130g candied fruits (whatever fruit you like)

1 tablespoon chopped chives

1. On a non-stick, lightly oiled hot pan, brown the scallops on both sides (1 minute each side).
2. Grill the black pudding.
3. Toss the fennel and apple in a bowl with the oil, vinegar, fennel seeds, vanilla, candied fruits and chives.
4. Season.

Oysters with tomato and ginger and horseradish mayonnaise

I was first introduced to this dish by a friend of mine, Matts Nordstrom, a great Swedish chef. He prepared this dish when he was guest chef at l'Ecrivain. I was so impressed . . . wow. Thanks, Matts.

For the oysters

24 oysters

4 large plum tomatoes (peeled, deseeded and diced)

100g fresh root ginger (peeled and diced)

2 tablespoons chopped coriander

1 red onion (diced)

25g brown sugar

For the horseradish mayonnaise

150ml mayonnaise

200g freshly grated horseradish (or 2 tbsp prepared horseradish sauce)

juice of 1 lemon

For the oysters

1. Opening oysters requires practice and can be dangerous, as the knife can slip. To prevent injury, hold the oyster with a thick cloth to protect your hand.
2. Insert a knife with a rigid, sharp, short blade (preferably an oyster knife) into the hinge of the shell and twist the knife to prise open the shell.
3. Remove the oyster from the shell and wash the shell.
4. Mix the tomato, ginger, coriander, onion and sugar in a bowl and season.
5. Spoon into the empty oyster shells and place a fresh oyster on top of each shell.

For the horseradish mayonnaise

1. Mix the mayonnaise with half the horseradish and the lemon juice. Season.
2. Spoon a little sauce over each oyster and sprinkle with the remaining horseradish.

Leabharlanna Dhún Laoghaire · Ráth An Dúin

Shellfish marinière

This is really just an adaptation of mussels marinière. It's a very, very simple one-pot wonder. You simply put all the ingredients into a pot and put it on the heat. Once cooked, it should be served immediately, so why not bring it to the table in the pot?

100g butter

1 onion (diced)

2 cloves garlic (sliced)

1 carrot (peeled and diced)

1 bulb fennel (diced)

1 stick celery (diced)

1 tablespoon paprika

100ml cream

200ml white wine

520g mussels with shells
   (cleaned)

260g clams

130g prawns

130g crab claws

4 lobster claws

1 bunch dill (chopped)

1. Melt the butter in a large shallow pan.
2. Sweat the onion, garlic, carrot, fennel and celery until soft but not browned.
3. Add the paprika, cream and wine. Season.
4. Add all the shellfish and cover the pan.
5. Simmer for 5 minutes, or until the mussel and clam shells have opened.
6. Sprinkle with the dill and serve immediately.

Tempura of tiger prawns with red onion and tomato salsa and wasabi mayonnaise

The secret to good tempura is to use chilled sparkling water. Any fish can be used in this recipe (monkfish, cod, etc.) as an alternative to prawns. The prawns must be cooked just before serving. Fry one prawn first to check that the batter is of the correct consistency. You may need to add more water or flour to adjust it. The spicy wasabi and salsa really complement each other.

For the tempura batter
iced sparkling water
100g cornflour

For the salsa
2 vine-ripened tomatoes (diced)
6 cherry tomatoes (halved)
1 red onion (finely sliced)
1 bunch coriander (chopped)
1 clove garlic (chopped)
1 red chilli (deseeded and diced)
olive oil
juice of 1 lime

For the wasabi mayonnaise
2 tablespoons mayonnaise
1 teaspoon wasabi paste

For the prawns
20 tiger prawns (shelled)
sieved flour
vegetable oil, for deep frying

For the tempura batter
1. In a large bowl, gradually whisk the sparkling water with the cornflour until a very light, airy batter is achieved.

For the salsa
1. Mix all the ingredients together in a bowl. Season to taste.

For the wasabi mayonnaise
1. Stir the mayonnaise and wasabi paste together in a bowl.

For the prawns
1. Coat the prawns in flour and dip in the batter.
2. Heat the oil in a pan. Add the prawns one at a time to the hot oil and fry until golden brown.
3. Place on sheets of kitchen towel to absorb excess oil.
4. Season to taste.

To serve
Place the prawns in a large bowl, and serve the wasabi mayonnaise and salsa in two smaller bowls.

6

elon salad · Apricot Melba · Rhubarb, orange and blackberry fool · Macerated winter fruits with honey crème fraîche · Pears poached in port ne · Lemon pudding · Eton mess · Banoffi sundae · Cranberry and intreau trifle with mascarpone cheese · Apple and berry strudel · Upside down pineapple tart · Individual Black rest gateaux · Baked blueberry and lime cheesecake · Irish apple and clove pie with whiskey cream · Toffee stard · Bread and butter pudding · Mocha mousse with sable and chocolate sauce · Chocolate pavé · Melon ad · Apricot Melba · Rhubarb, orange and blackberry fool · Macerated winter fruits with honey crème fraîche · ars poached in port wine · Lemon pudding · Eton mess · Banoffi sundae · Cranberry and Cointreau trifle with scarpone cheese · Apple and berry strudel · Upside down pineapple tart · Individual Black Forest gateaux

Dessert

Melon salad

This is very simple and ideal for a hot summer day. Chill all the ingredients. The salad looks brilliant when served in a large glass bowl in the centre of the table. I am using it here as a dessert, but adding some Parma ham turns it into a great starter.

1 honeydew melon

1 small watermelon

1 Galia melon

3 tablespoons honey

200ml orange juice

fresh mint

200g natural yoghurt

zest of 1 lime

icing sugar, to taste

1. Cut the melon flesh into whatever shapes you like.
2. Mix the honey and orange juice together and finely chop the mint.
3. Combine the yoghurt, lime zest and icing sugar, checking for sweetness.
4. Toss the melon and mint in the orange dressing and serve with a dollop of lime yoghurt.

Apricot Melba

Using seasonal produce is always good, so why not try this dish when apricots are in season? It's a new twist on peach Melba, which is a timeless classic and a very popular dish.

150ml water

100g sugar

4 apricots

100ml cream, plus extra to serve

1 vanilla pod

40g icing sugar

2 punnets raspberries

1. Prepare a stock syrup by boiling the water with the sugar in a heavy-based pan.
2. Halve the apricots and remove the pits.
3. When the syrup comes to the boil, add the apricots and cook until they become soft.
4. Whip the cream, vanilla and 20g icing sugar together.
5. Blitz 1 punnet of raspberries with the other 20g of icing sugar. Sieve to make a purée.

To assemble

1. Serve in glasses, layering the apricot, raspberry and cream.
2. Top off with a layer of whipped cream and a few of the remaining raspberries.

Rhubarb, orange and blackberry fool

This looks fabulous served in a glass. When rhubarb is not in season, you could use your choice of berries instead. If the rhubarb is sour, add some sugar to sweeten it.

7 large stalks pink rhubarb
    (washed and chopped)
sugar, to taste
vanilla extract, to taste
300ml cream
200g natural yoghurt
4 oranges (peeled and
    segmented)
1 punnet blackberries

1. Stew the rhubarb in a pot over a high heat with 2 tbsp water, sugar and vanilla extract. Allow to cool.
2. Whip the cream, then fold it into the rhubarb along with the yoghurt.
3. Layer up four glasses with rhubarb fool, then orange segments and berries, until the glasses are three-quarters full.

To serve
If you like, top with cookies, wafers or grated chocolate.

Rhubarb and ginger crumble

Everybody loves crumble. Rhubarb and ginger is a real wow combination. I feel it must be served warm. It's nice to serve with ice cream to enjoy the hot and cold taste sensation.

10 rhubarb stalks

8 tbsp caster sugar

4 tbsp water

1 knob of fresh ginger (peeled and finely grated)

100g butter (softened)

100g Demerara sugar

180–200g plain flour

ice cream (to serve)

1. Preheat the oven to 180°C.
2. Cut the rhubarb into 8cm slices, discarding any leaves. Place on an oven tray.
3. Sprinkle the sugar and water over the rhubarb.
4. Add the ginger to the mixture.
5. Cook in the oven for 10 minutes. Transfer the rhubarb to an ovenproof dish.
6. In a bowl, mix the butter and Demerara sugar together until the mixture resembles breadcrumbs.
7. Add the flour to make the crumble topping.
8. Sprinkle the crumble mixture over the rhubarb.
9. Bake in the oven for 30–40 minutes, until golden brown.
10. Serve warm, with ice cream.

Macerated winter fruits with honey crème fraîche

What a great way to use dried fruits, which most people always have in the larder. This is perfect as an emergency dessert. The dish could also be made with your choice of fresh stoned fruit. The honey in the crème fraîche is optional.

100g dried apricots
100g dried or fresh figs
100g dried dates
200g dried cranberries

For the syrup

1 bottle red wine
150g sugar
zest and juice of 1 orange
200ml orange juice
1 cinnamon stick
a few cloves

For the honey crème fraîche

3 tbsp honey
200g crème fraîche

1. Bring the wine, sugar, orange zest and juice and spices to the boil and simmer until the sugar has dissolved.
2. Take off the heat, add the dried fruit and leave to soak for a few hours.
3. Either reheat the fruit or serve cold.
4. Just before serving, add the honey to the crème fraîche and add a dollop of crème fraîche to each serving.

Pears poached in port wine

The pears in this dish take on a lovely rich burgundy colour. The cinnamon makes it quite a wintery dessert. Serve warm or cold: either is delicious.

6 firm, green, slightly under-ripe
   pears with stalks
120g caster sugar
280ml red wine
140ml port
8 star anise
2 cinnamon sticks
2 vanilla beans
zest of 1 lemon or 1 orange

1. Peel the pears and take a thin slice off the bottom of each so that you can stand it upright.
2. Place the pears into a high-sided saucepan that will hold them tightly; it should not be deep enough for them to float.
3. Put all the other ingredients into the saucepan and top up with water to reach just below the pear stalks.
4. Bring to the boil, cover with a lid and reduce the heat to a simmer.
5. Poach for 30–45 minutes, or until the pears are tender. How long this takes will depend on their variety and ripeness.
6. Leave to cool slightly, then carefully remove the pears to a shallow dish.
7. Bring the syrup to the boil again and reduce until it is think enough to coat the back of a spoon.
8. Allow the syrup to cool and pour it over the pears.
9. Chill, spooning the syrup over the pears from time to time.

Lemon pudding

I think everybody loves steamed pudding, and lemon is probably the most popular of all. This dessert can be a little dry, so it is best served with some cream or ice cream.

125g plain flour

1 teaspoon baking powder

175g caster sugar

125g butter, plus extra for greasing

2 eggs

zest and juice of 2 lemons

1 tablespoon milk

shop-bought lemon curd, to serve

cream or ice cream, to serve

1. Lightly grease 4–6 individual pudding moulds.
2. Bring a kettle of water to the boil.
3. Sift the flour and baking powder together into a bowl.
4. In a separate bowl, cream the sugar and butter thoroughly until smooth and fluffy.
5. Beat in the eggs.
6. Add the lemon zest and juice, then sprinkle the flour and baking powder into the mixture. Beat again until mixed.
7. Add a little milk to slacken the mixture to a dropping consistency, but don't let the mix become sloppy.
8. Spoon the mixture into pudding moulds.
9. Cover the moulds tightly with foil to prevent steam from escaping when they are cooking. Using lengths of string, secure the foil under the rims.
10. Put the moulds into a roasting tray and pour in enough boiling water to come halfway up the sides of the moulds. Steam for about 40–50 minutes at 140°C, topping up regularly with boiling water.
11. Take the moulds out and turn out the puddings while hot (they will come out of the moulds more easily if they are still hot).
12. Serve with lemon curd and cream or ice cream.

Eton mess

This is a great way to use up any broken meringues you might have. It's a really simple, sweet, crunchy and moreish dessert.

175 caster sugar (measured out before you begin)

3 large egg whites

2 punnets fresh strawberries (hulled and chopped)

1 rounded tablespoon icing sugar

570ml cream (whipped until floppy)

1. Preheat the oven to 150°C.
2. Line a baking tray with non-stick silicone paper (parchment).
3. Place the egg whites in a scrupulously clean bowl and whisk until they form soft peaks that slightly tip over when you lift the whisk.
4. Add the caster sugar about a tablespoon at a time and continue to whisk until each tablespoon of sugar has been thoroughly incorporated.
5. Place rounded dessertspoonfuls of the mixture in rows on the lined baking tray.
6. Place the baking tray on the centre shelf of the oven.
7. Turn the heat down to 140°C. After 1 hour, turn the oven off and leave the meringues in the oven to dry out overnight, or until the oven is completely cold.

To make strawberry purée

1. Place half the strawberries in a blender together with the icing sugar. Whiz to a purée.
2. Pass the purée through a sieve to remove the seeds.

To serve

1. Roughly break up the meringues into irregular pieces and place them in a large mixing bowl.
2. Add the chopped strawberries, then fold in the cream.
3. Gently fold in all but about 2 tablespoons of the strawberry purée to give a marbled effect.
4. Pile the whole lot into a serving dish, drizzle the rest of the strawberry purée over the top and serve immediately.

Banoffi sundae

Banoffi can sometimes be a little heavy. This recipe gives you the same great flavours, but is lighter than the conventional version.

200g brown sugar

50g butter

400ml cream

4 digestive biscuits

2 bananas

1. Place the sugar in a heavy-bottomed saucepan.
2. Melt over a high heat to make a caramel.
3. Add the butter and half the cream.
4. Stir and allow to come to the boil.
5. Turn the heat down and cook, stirring occasionally, until you have a fairly thick fudge sauce (about 15 minutes).
6. Leave to cool.
7. Whip the rest of the cream to soft peaks.
8. Crumble the biscuits into two sundae glasses.
9. Drizzle over a little of the toffee sauce.
10. Peel and slice the bananas and place half of the slices on top of the biscuits.
11. Toss the remaining banana slices in a little lemon juice to stop them from going brown.
12. Add the cream to the glasses, then the remaining bananas and toffee sauce.

Cranberry and Cointreau trifle with mascarpone cheese

For the trifle

juice of 1 orange

130g caster sugar

1 vanilla pod

60g cranberries soaked in
  1 shot of Cointreau

1 shot Cointreau, for flaming

12 sponge fingers

1 packet raspberry jelly

1 medium (150–200ml) tub
  mascarpone cheese

200ml crème anglaise (recipe
  on p. 162) or custard

For the frosted cranberries

150ml water

100g sugar, plus extra for
  dipping the cranberries

chocolate shavings, to decorate

For the trifle

1. Heat a small saucepan. Add the orange juice, sugar, vanilla pod and cranberries. Simmer for 5 minutes.
2. Flame the Cointreau with a match to burn off the alcohol. Add to the cranberries.
3. Taste and add more sugar if needed.
4. Strain off the liquid and allow to cool.
5. Use this liquid to soak the sponge fingers.

For the frosted cranberries

1. Prepare a stock syrup by boiling the water with the sugar in a heavy-based pan.
2. Dip the cranberries in the stock syrup, then in the sugar.

To serve

1. Begin with a layer of sponge fingers.
2. Make up the raspberry jelly and immediately pour the jelly over the sponge fingers. Leave to set.
3. Add the cooked cranberries, then a layer of custard.
4. Top with mascarpone cheese.
5. Sprinkle with chocolate shavings and frosted cranberries.

Apple and berry strudel

This dessert is ideal for using up slightly over-ripe apples and berries. Having the pastry in the freezer means that you can rustle this up if you find yourself stuck for a dessert. I prefer this dessert served hot.

50g raspberries

50g blackberries

50g blueberries

1 glass port

2 large apples (peeled, cored and roughly chopped)

100g sugar

50g raisins

2 cinnamon sticks

5 pieces star anise

2 sheets filo pastry

75g butter (melted)

1. Marinate the berries in the port for 12 hours.
2. Add the apple to a pan with the sugar, raisins, cinnamon and star anise and simmer until soft.
3. Drain the port from the berries, then fold the berries through the apple. Mix and leave to one side.
4. Brush the filo pastry with melted butter.
5. Put the apple mix in the middle of the filo pastry.
6. Fold the filo over into a parcel.
7. Brush the top with melted butter.
8. Bake in the oven at 150°C until golden brown.

Upside down pineapple tart

Pineapple, which is easy to source all year round, naturally contains a lot of sugar. This is a very simple dessert that looks well. I would serve it with cream, ice cream or crème fraîche.

200g caster sugar

25g butter

1 pineapple

1 pack ready-made puff pastry

1 tbsp icing sugar

1. Preheat the oven to 200°C.
2. Put the sugar in an ovenproof, flameproof pan and heat gently without stirring until it caramelises and turns golden brown.
3. Remove from the heat, add the butter and stir in gently.
4. Peel and slice the pineapple and place the slices in a single layer on the caramel.
5. Roll out the puff pastry on a lightly floured surface.
6. Cut out a disc (or whatever shape fits your pan) slightly larger than the pan.
7. Place the pastry over the pineapple and caramel.
8. Tuck the edges of the pastry into the sides of the pan.
9. Bake for 15–20 minutes, until the pastry is brown.
10. Remove the tart from the oven and set aside to rest for 4 minutes.
11. Place a serving plate on top of the pan and invert it, so that the tart slips out with the pastry on the base and the pineapple on top.
12. Dust with icing sugar.

Individual
Black Forest gateaux

Black Forest gateaux were seen a lot more often in the past than they are now. This dessert is often considered to be quite heavy, but when the gateaux are prepared correctly, they really are delicious and light. Tinned cherries can be used in this dish, but of course fresh cherries are best if possible.

For the chocolate sponge
340g unsalted butter,
    plus extra for greasing
340g caster sugar
6 eggs
240g self-raising flour (sifted)
100g cocoa powder (sifted)

For the filling
100g sugar
100ml water
2 measures kirsch
250g fresh cherries (halved
    and pitted)
100ml whipped cream
seeds from 1 vanilla pod
icing sugar, to taste
200g good-quality chocolate

For the chocolate sponge
1. Preheat the oven to 170°C.
2. Cream the butter and sugar until light and fluffy.
3. Slowly add the eggs, then fold in the sifted flour and cocoa powder.
4. Pour into a greased cake tin and bake for 20–30 minutes, or until a skewer put into the cake comes out clean.
5. Take the cake out and turn onto a wire rack to cool.
6. When cooled, slice the cake twice horizontally so you have three thin cakes. Using a pastry cutter, cut out 12 rings (three sponge rings for each gateau).

For the filling
1. Make a stock syrup by boiling together the sugar, water and kirsch.
2. When the sugar has dissolved, add the cherries and bring back to the boil.
3. Take off the heat and allow the cherries to cool.
4. Whip the cream to soft peaks with the vanilla seeds and icing sugar to taste.
5. Grate the chocolate on the fine side of a grater.

To assemble the gateaux

1. Sprinkle the sponges with some of the liquid from the cherries.

2. Take a ring or large pastry cutter and place in it first a layer of sponge, then a small amount of cream, then a layer of cherries and some more cream.

3. Repeat this layering process once more and top with a third piece of sponge.

4. Push down lightly on the sponge to make sure the gateau is compact. Remove the ring.

5. Top the gateau with some more cream and decorate with a few cherries and some grated chocolate.

6. Repeat this process for the other three gateaux.

Baked blueberry and lime cheesecake

I much prefer the flavour of baked cheesecake to fridge-set cheesecake, which can be quite gelatinous. This cake can be topped with any fruit of your choice, or indeed served plain.

For the base
180g digestive biscuits
45g butter (melted and cooled)

For the filling
125g butter
75g caster sugar
½ tsp vanilla extract
2 large eggs (separated)
500g cream cheese (at room temperature)

For the topping
2 punnets blueberries
100g sugar
zest of 1 lime

For the base
1. Grease the sides and line the base of a 23cm springform cake tin.
2. Crush the digestive biscuits into fine crumbs.
3. Stir in the cooled melted butter and mix well to combine.
4. Press into the base of the prepared tin.
5. Refrigerate while you prepare the filling.

For the filling
1. Cream the butter and sugar together with the vanilla extract until fluffy. Beat in the egg yolks.
2. Add the softened cream cheese and beat again.
3. Whisk the egg whites until just stiff and fold into the mixture. Pour onto the biscuit base.
4. Bake in a moderately low oven at 160°C for 1¼ hours. When cooked, turn off the oven, leaving the cheesecake to cool in the oven.

For the topping
1. Put the blueberries, sugar and lime zest in a saucepan.
2. Heat until the fruit just comes to the boil – don't allow the blueberries to break up.
3. Take off the heat and leave to cool.
4. When the cheesecake and blueberries are cool, remove the cheesecake from the tin. Cut into slices, top with the blueberries and serve.

Irish apple pie
with whiskey cream

When I was a kid, this was always the way apple pie was made: with cloves, on a plate and then into the oven. The aromas and flavours released by the cloves during cooking adds so much to a simple apple pie. If you don't have time to make the pastry, you can always use ready-made sweet pastry.

250g caster sugar
500g flour
250g butter
2 eggs (lightly whisked)
4–6 cooking apples (peeled, cored and cut into eights)
100g brown sugar, plus a little extra
4 cloves

For the whiskey cream
100ml cream
1 measure whiskey
icing sugar, to taste

1. Put the sugar and flour into a bowl and mix with your hands. Cut the butter into small cubes and add it to the flour and sugar mixture.
2. Rub in the butter with your fingers until the mixture reaches the consistency of crumbs, then add the eggs and mix until the mixture comes together to form a smooth dough. Put in the fridge for 20 minutes.
3. Mix the apples in a bowl with the brown sugar and cloves and set aside.
4. Roll out the pastry and cut into two circles using a plate and a knife. Make one of the circles slightly bigger than the other.
5. Line an ovenproof plate or pie dish with the smaller circle of pastry, then add the apple mixture.
6. Egg wash the rim of the pastry and cover the top with the bigger circle of pastry. Press a fork all the way round the edge of the pie, make a small hole in the centre and sprinkle the top with brown sugar.
7. Bake in the oven at 150°C for about 20–30 minutes, or until golden brown.

For the whiskey cream
1. Whip the cream with the whiskey and icing sugar until soft peaks form.

Toffee custard

Crème caramel, or toffee custard, as I call it here, was the very first dish I ever prepared in a restaurant kitchen. I prefer this dessert to crème brulée and it is less expensive to make. Always make sure the caramel is nice and brown. Instead of making individual servings, you could always make one large dessert.

For the caramel

150g sugar

50ml water

For the custard base

500ml milk

vanilla pod (optional)

4 whole eggs

1 egg yolk

120g sugar

For the caramel

1. Place the sugar and water in a heavy-based saucepan.
2. Slowly mix the sugar and water together over a low heat until the sugar has dissolved.
3. Turn up the heat. Do not mix or stir.
4. Leave until the mixture becomes caramel coloured.
5. Take off the heat to avoid burning the caramel.
6. Pour the caramel into individual moulds (or one large mould).
7. Heat the oven to 140°C.

For the custard base

1. Place the milk and vanilla pod in a saucepan and heat until it just comes to the boil.
2. Whisk the eggs and yolk with the sugar and pour slowly into the milk.
3. Whisk continuously until the eggs are completely incorporated into the milk.
4. Sieve the mixture and pour into the moulds.
5. Place the moulds in a large roasting tray and fill the tray with boiling water to halfway up the moulds.
6. Bake in the oven at 140°C for 40 minutes.
7. Allow to cool before turning out of the moulds.

Bread and butter pudding

Bread and butter pudding is a great way to use up bread that has gone slightly past its best. For a twist, you could use brioche or croissants in place of bread. The combination of sultanas and nutmeg (or cinnamon) make this pudding very tasty. Always serve this warm, with custard. A dash of Baileys will give the custard a bit of a kick.

8 slices white bread

50g butter (more if required)

50g sultanas

ground nutmeg or cinnamon

2 eggs

450ml full-fat milk

50g granulated sugar

custard (to serve)

1. Remove the crusts from the bread.
2. Butter each slice on one side only and cut into triangles.
3. Use some of the butter to grease an ovenproof dish.
4. Cover the base of the dish with one layer of bread triangles, laying the buttered side down.
5. Sprinkle some of the sultanas on the bread with a little nutmeg or cinnamon.
6. Repeat with another layer of bread, sultanas and spice, finishing with a layer of bread with the buttered side up.
7. Beat the eggs with the milk and sugar and pour over the bread layers.
8. Let the pudding sit for 30 minutes so that the bread soaks up the liquid.
9. Bake at 180°C for about 30 minutes or until golden and puffy.
10. Serve warm with custard.

Mocha mousse with sables and chocolate sauce

This is a deliciously light recipe for people who find chocolate too rich and heavy at the end of a meal. It looks great layered in a glass and topped with the mascarpone.

For the mousse

100g whole eggs
    (about 3 eggs: 1 egg = 40g)
6 egg yolks
50g sugar
1 shot espresso
150g plain chocolate
2 leaves gelatine
250ml whipped cream

For the sable

225g chocolate
225g butter
300g cream flour

For the chocolate sauce

250ml cream
200g plain chocolate (chopped)

Chantilly cream (to serve)

For the mousse

1. Whisk the egg and egg yolks.
2. Make a stock syrup by boiling the sugar with a little water. Add the espresso. Pour the stock syrup onto the egg mix and whisk until light and fluffy.
3. Melt the chocolate, either in a bowl over simmering water or in the microwave.
4. Soak the gelatine in warm water. When it has softened, strain off the water. Mix the chocolate and gelatine into the egg mixture. Fold in the cream.

For the sable

1. Blend all the ingredients in a blender until the mix forms a dough. Rest the mix in the fridge for 4 hours.
2. Roll out the mixture thinly (about the thickness of a coin).
3. Cook in a preheated oven at 140˚C for 20–30 minutes, or until golden brown.
4. Allow to cool, then crush to form a crumble.

For the chocolate sauce

1. Bring the cream to the boil, pour onto the chocolate and stir.

To serve

1. Spoon the mousse into martini/cocktail glasses, drizzle with chocolate sauce and top with the crumbled sable.
2. Leave the glasses in the fridge until ready to serve.
3. Serve with Chantilly cream.

Chocolate pavé

This is a delicious, luscious dessert, ideal for chocolate lovers. Soaking the sponge in the crème de cassis gives a great flavour. Serve with caramelised bananas to really spoil your guests.

2 whole eggs

5 egg yolks

250g sugar

80ml water

300g dark chocolate (melted)

500ml whipped cream

store-bought chocolate sponge
  for the base

1 shot crème de cassis

1. Whisk the eggs and yolks in a bowl over a saucepan of simmering water.
2. Continue to whisk until the mixture is fluffy, light in colour and holds its shape when you pass the whisk through it in a figure eight.
3. Heat the sugar and water until it reaches 110°C (if you are using a sugar thermometer) or to the soft ball stage (just before it browns).
4. Gently pour the sugar and water over the egg mixture and continue to whisk.
5. Fold in the melted chocolate and then fold in the cream.
6. Break the chocolate sponge into pieces and use them to line the bottom of a baking tray. Drizzle the crème de cassis (or liquor of your choice) over the sponge.
7. Pour the chocolate mixture over the sponge and refrigerate overnight, until set.

ef or veal stock · Chicken stock · Duck stock · Fish stock ·
ngoustine stock · Vegetable stock · Beurre blanc · Beurre rouge
Jus · Pasta · Risotto · Mayonnaise · Aïoli · Froth · Puff pastry ·
onge cake · Crème anglaise · Stock syrup · Beef or veal stock · Chicken stock · Duck stock · Fish stock
Langoustine stock · Vegetable stock · Beurre blanc · Beurre rouge · Jus · Pasta · Risotto · Mayonnaise
Aïoli · Froth · Puff pastry · Sponge cake · Crème anglaise · Stock syrup · Beef or veal stock · Chicken
ck · Duck stock · Fish stock · Langoustine stock · Vegetable stock · Beurre blanc · Beurre rouge · Jus
Pasta · Risotto · Mayonnaise · Aïoli · Froth · Puff pastry · Sponge cake · Crème anglaise · Stock
rup · Beef or veal stock · Chicken stock · Duck stock · Fish stock · Langoustine stock · Vegetable stock

Chef's Staples

The following recipes are the building blocks of many good dishes.

Beef or veal stock

Makes about 1½–2 litres

2kg beef (or veal) bones
1 bay leaf
2 parsley stalks
1 sprig thyme
40g butter
1 large onion (unpeeled, roughly chopped)
3 medium carrots (unpeeled, roughly chopped)
2 medium leeks (roughly chopped)
2 sticks celery (roughly chopped)
60g mushroom trimmings (roughly chopped)
1 tomato (roughly chopped)
1 clove garlic (unpeeled)
3 white peppercorns
8 litres water

1. Preheat the oven to 200°C.
2. Arrange the bones on a roasting tin and roast for 1 hour.
3. Tie the bay leaf, parsley and thyme together with string to make a bouquet garni.
4. Melt the butter in a large saucepan and colour the onion, carrots, leeks and celery in the butter before adding the roasted bones (drained of excess fat), the bouquet garni, mushroom trimmings, tomato, garlic and peppercorns.
5. Add the water, bring to the boil and skim the scum from the surface using a ladle.
6. Reduce the heat and simmer very gently, uncovered, for 8–9 hours, continuing to skim any scum from the surface.
7. Pass through a fine sieve into a large bowl, discarding any solids. Cool, cover and refrigerate.
8. The stock will keep for 5 days in the fridge.
9. Stock can be frozen in ice cube trays and stored in plastic bags in the freezer.

Chicken stock

Makes about 1½ litres

1 bay leaf
1 parsley stalk
1 sprig thyme
3 raw chicken carcases (skin and fat removed)
about 2½ litres water
1 large carrot (trimmed and quartered)
1 medium leek (roughly chopped)
2 sticks celery (roughly chopped)
1 large onion (unpeeled and roughly chopped)
3 white peppercorns

1. Tie the bay leaf, parsley stalk and thyme together with string to make a bouquet garni.
2. Place the chicken carcases in a large saucepan and cover with water. Bring to the boil and skim any scum from the surface with a ladle.
3. Add all the other ingredients and simmer the stock, uncovered, very gently for 4 hours.
4. Strain the stock through a fine sieve. Discard the bones, vegetables and herbs.
5. Cool and refrigerate in a covered container. The stock will keep for more than a week in the fridge.
6. Stock can be frozen in ice cube trays and stored in plastic bags in the freezer.

Duck stock

Makes about 500ml

600g duck bones

200ml red wine

1½ litres water

1 sprig thyme

1 bay leaf

2 parsley stalks

1 small carrot (peeled and
roughly chopped)

1 small onion (roughly chopped)

1 stick celery (roughly chopped)

1 sprig sage

1 sprig rosemary

2 juniper berries (crushed)

½ clove garlic (crushed)

2 tablespoons olive oil

30 dried mushrooms, soaked
for 20 minutes

2 white peppercorns

1. Preheat the oven to 200˚C.
2. Place the bones in a roasting tin and roast until
   they are really brown.
3. Remove the bones from the oven and transfer them
   to a large saucepan.
4. Deglaze the roasting tin with the wine and add this
   to the saucepan along with the water.
5. Bring to the boil and remove any scum from the
   surface with a ladle.
6. Tie the thyme, bay leaf and parsley together with
   string to make a bouquet garni.
7. Place the vegetables, sage, rosemary, juniper berries
   and garlic in a roasting tin and drizzle with the oil.
8. Roast in the oven for about 20 minutes, until the
   vegetables are soft and brown but not burned.
9. Add the vegetables and herbs to the stock with the
   bouquet garni, dried mushrooms and peppercorns.
10. Simmer gently, uncovered, for 4 hours.
11. Strain the stock through a fine sieve. Discard the
    bones, vegetables and herbs. Cool and refrigerate
    in a covered container.
12. The stock will keep for 2–3 days in the fridge.
13. Stock can be frozen in ice cube trays and stored in
    plastic bags in the freezer.

Fish stock

Makes about 1½ litres

40g butter
1 medium onion (roughly
  chopped)
1 bay leaf
4 white peppercorns
10 parsley stalks
juice of ½ lemon
1.5kg fish bones (sole, turbot
  or whiting), washed
1½ litres water

1. Melt the butter in a large saucepan. Add the onion, bay leaf, peppercorns, parsley stalks, lemon juice and fish bones and cook gently for 5 minutes.

2. Add the water, bring the stock to the boil and skim off any scum with a ladle. Lower the heat and simmer for 20 minutes.

3. Strain through a fine sieve and use at once or cool and refrigerate in a covered container for no more than 1 day.

4. Stock can be frozen in ice cube trays and stored in plastic bags in the freezer.

Langoustine stock

Makes about 2 litres

3kg langoustine/prawn shells
75g butter
2 medium onions (roughly
   chopped)
2 medium carrots (peeled and
   roughly chopped)
2 sticks celery (roughly chopped)
2 medium leeks (roughly
   chopped)
1 fennel bulb (roughly chopped)
200ml white wine
100ml brandy
1 stalk lemongrass
1 bay leaf
8 white peppercorns
20g parsley stalks
2 tablespoons tomato paste
5 litres water

1. Preheat the oven to 150˚C.
2. Roast the langoustine/prawn shells until golden brown.
3. Heat the butter in a large saucepan and cook the vegetables until they are golden brown.
4. Add the wine to deglaze the saucepan, then add the roasted prawn shells and flambé with the brandy by pouring the brandy into the saucepan and lighting it. (Pour the brandy from a separate container, not the bottle, use a long match, and be prepared for a whoosh of flame.)
5. Add the lemongrass, bay leaf, peppercorns, parsley stalks, tomato paste and cold water.
6. Bring to the boil and simmer gently for 2 hours, skimming any scum from the surface with a ladle.
7. Pass through a fine sieve into a large bowl, discarding any solids. Cool, cover and refrigerate.
8. The stock will keep for 2–3 days in the fridge.
9. Stock can be frozen in ice cube trays and stored in plastic bags in the freezer.

Vegetable stock

Makes about 1¼ litres

40g butter
1 large onion (unpeeled, roughly chopped)
2 carrots (unpeeled, roughly chopped)
4 sticks celery (roughly chopped)
2 leeks (roughly chopped)
1 parsnip (unpeeled, roughly chopped)
25g dried mushrooms, soaked for 20 minutes
1 tomato (roughly chopped)
1 clove garlic (sliced)
1 bay leaf
1 sprig thyme
5 white peppercorns
3 parsley stalks
pinch of salt
2 litres water

1. Melt the butter in a large saucepan and gently colour the onion, carrots, celery, leeks and parsnip before adding all the other ingredients.
2. Bring to the boil, reduce the heat and simmer, uncovered, for 30 minutes.
3. Remove the saucepan from the heat and let it sit for another 30 minutes.
4. Strain the stock through a fine sieve to remove all the solids.
5. Cool completely before refrigerating in a covered container.
6. The stock should be used within 2 days.
7. Stock can be frozen in ice cube trays and stored in plastic bags in the freezer.

Beurre blanc

2 shallots (finely chopped)
20ml white wine vinegar
40ml dry white wine
60ml fish stock or water
20ml cream
175g unsalted butter (diced)

1. Put the shallots in a small saucepan with the wine vinegar, wine and stock or water. Bring to the boil and simmer until nearly all the liquid has evaporated.
2. Add the cream and reduce a little.
3. Reduce the heat and add the butter piece by piece, whisking briskly, until all the butter is incorporated into the sauce and the sauce has thickened.
4. Serve at once.

Beurre rouge

2 red onions (finely chopped)
150ml red wine
85ml chicken stock
85ml red wine vinegar
½ teaspoon sugar
pinch of salt
100g unsalted butter (diced)

1. Put the onions in a medium-sized saucepan with the wine, chicken stock, red wine vinegar, sugar and salt.
2. Bring to the boil, reduce to a simmer and cook until the onions are soft.
3. Reduce the heat and add the butter piece by piece, whisking vigorously, until all the butter is incorporated into the sauce and the sauce has thickened.
4. Serve at once.

Jus

20g butter

1 shallot (chopped)

1 clove garlic (chopped)

1 stick celery (roughly chopped)

1 carrot (unpeeled and roughly chopped)

1 bay leaf

1 sprig thyme

1 tablespoon sugar

1 tablespoon balsamic vinegar

200ml ruby port

200ml red wine

1½–2 litres beef or veal stock

1. Melt the butter in a large saucepan and gently cook the shallot, garlic, celery, carrot, bay leaf and thyme for about 5 minutes.
2. Add the sugar and cook for 2–3 minutes to caramelise.
3. Add the balsamic vinegar, port and red wine and reduce by half.
4. Add the stock and reduce to a sauce consistency.
5. Pass through a muslin-lined sieve, cool and refrigerate in a covered container.

Pasta

500g 00 flour (sifted)

3 eggs

6 egg yolks

pinch of salt

1 tablespoon olive oil

1. Place the flour in a food processor. Add the eggs and egg yolks and process until the dough just starts to form a ball.
2. Add the salt and olive oil and combine.
3. Shake a little flour on a work surface and knead the ball of dough by hand for 5 minutes until it's smooth, adding more flour if it sticks.
4. Wrap the dough in clingfilm and rest it in a cool place for 1–2 hours.

Risotto

50g butter

1 small onion (peeled and
   finely diced)

300g Arborio rice

1 litre chicken stock
   (see p. 149)

salt and freshly ground white
   pepper

1. Melt the butter in a medium-sized saucepan and cook the onion gently for 5 minutes, until tender.
2. Add the rice, stir, and cook for another 3 minutes.
3. Meanwhile, heat the stock in a separate saucepan.
4. Add the hot stock to the rice ladle by ladle, stirring constantly.
5. Continue to stir, allowing the rice to simmer, until all the stock is absorbed (15–18 minutes) and the rice is cooked.
6. Season to taste.

Mayonnaise

2 egg yolks
1 tablespoon Dijon mustard
1 tablespoon white wine vinegar
salt and freshly ground white
    pepper
300ml olive oil

1. Combine the egg yolks, mustard, vinegar and seasoning in a food processor.
2. Blend for 1 minute before slowly drizzling in the olive oil.
3. Continue to slowly add the oil until the sauce reaches a thick mayonnaise consistency.
4. Adjust the seasoning and refrigerate.
5. Mayonnaise will keep for 2 days in the fridge.

Aïoli

4 cloves garlic (crushed)
2 egg yolks
250ml olive oil
salt and freshly ground white
    pepper
1 tablespoon lemon juice

1. Combine the garlic with the egg yolks in a food processor.
2. Blend for 1 minute before slowly drizzling in the olive oil.
3. Continue to add the oil slowly until the aïoli has taken on the consistency of mayonnaise.
4. Season with salt and pepper, then add the lemon juice and taste again. Refrigerate.
5. Aïoli will keep for 2 days in the fridge.

Froth

90ml vegetable stock
90ml cream
salt and freshly ground white
 pepper
50g butter (diced)

1. Bring the vegetable stock to the boil in a medium-sized saucepan and simmer until it has reduced by half.
2. Add 60ml of the cream and reduce again by half. Season and pass through a sieve.
3. Add the remaining cream and, using a balloon whisk or hand-held blender, whisk in the butter and froth the mixture until you have a good foam.
4. Spoon the foam onto the plate when you are ready to serve.

Puff pastry

500g strong white flour (sifted)

pinch of salt

500g unsalted butter

1 teaspoon lemon juice

250–300ml cold water

1. Place the flour in a large bowl and add the salt.
2. Rub 50g of the butter into the flour, then add the lemon juice and enough water to make a soft dough that does not stick to the bowl.
3. Knead to a smooth dough.
4. Roll the dough into a ball and wrap in clingfilm.
5. Refrigerate for 30 minutes.
6. Cut a cross in the ball of dough, then pull out the four corners in the shape of a star, leaving the centre about 15mm thick.
7. Roll out each corner to a quarter the thickness of the centre.
8. Knead the rest of the butter and place it in the centre of the pastry. Fold over the corners and enclose the butter completely, excluding any air.
9. Fold the pastry in three and roll it out in the opposite direction to the way it was rolled previously, then fold in three again.
10. Wrap the dough in clingfilm and refrigerate for 30 minutes.
11. Repeat the rolling and folding procedure twice more. Rest the pastry for 1 hour before using.

Sponge cake

4 medium eggs, beaten

110g caster sugar

1 tablespoon vegetable oil

110g self-raising flour (sifted)

1. Preheat the oven to 180°C.
2. Whisk the eggs and sugar together in a bowl until light and fluffy, then add the oil.
3. Fold in the flour gently and pour the mixture into a 28cm round cake tin. Bake for 25 minutes, until golden brown.
4. Cool on a wire rack.

Crème anglaise

300ml cream

100ml milk

1 vanilla pod (halved
   lengthways)

4 egg yolks

80g caster sugar

1. Bring the cream, milk and vanilla pod to the boil in a large saucepan.
2. Meanwhile, whisk the egg yolks and caster sugar in a heatproof bowl over a large saucepan of simmering water until the mixture is pale and creamy.
3. When the cream mixture starts to boil, pour it slowly over the egg and sugar mixture, whisking all the time.
4. Transfer the mixture back into the saucepan the cream was heated in and continue cooking on a gentle heat until the custard coats the back of a wooden spoon.
5. Pass the custard through a sieve.
6. Scrape the seeds from the vanilla pod into the custard, then discard the pod.
7. Allow to cool.

Stock syrup

450g sugar

570ml water

80g liquid glucose

1. Place all the ingredients in a large saucepan.
2. Stir, without heating, until the sugar has dissolved, then bring the mixture to the boil.
3. Take off the heat and allow to cool.

8

hardonnay · Chenin Blanc · Gewürztraminer · Pinot Gris/Pinot
rigio · Riesling · Sauvignon Blanc · Sémillon · Cabernet
auvignon and blends · Merlot · Pinot Noir · Sangiovese · Syrah/Shiraz
Tempranillo · Rosé · Chenin Blanc · Riesling · Sémillon · Tokaji · Port · Sherry · Non-vintage champagne
Vintage champagne · Cava · Prosecco · Asti · New World sparkling wine · English sparkling wine ·
hardonnay · Chenin Blanc · Gewürztraminer · Pinot Gris/Pinot Grigio · Riesling · Sauvignon Blanc · Sémillon
Cabernet Sauvignon and blends · Merlot · Pinot Noir · Sangiovese · Syrah/Shiraz · Tempranillo · Rosé
Chenin Blanc · Riesling · Sémillon · Tokaji · Port · Sherry · Non-vintage champagne · Vintage champagne
Cava · Prosecco · Asti · New World sparkling wine · Chardonnay · Chenin Blanc · Gewürztraminer

Guide to Matching Wine and Food

To help you choose wines that will complement the recipes in the book, we have given a very general outline of the most popular grape varieties. Wines made from the same grape varieties can vary tremendously, depending on the country and region where they're grown. Wines from warmer climates tend to be richer and fuller bodied than wines from cooler areas.

Sometimes more than one wine can go with a recipe – it all depends on personal preference. The 'Old World' refers to Europe and the 'New World' covers North and South America, Australia, New Zealand and South Africa.

Dry whites

Chardonnay

The best-known white grape variety. Chardonnay styles vary dramatically, depending on whether the wine has been matured in oak barrels or stainless steel vats. Unoaked chardonnay, such as Chablis, has a mineral steeliness and quite high acidity, with green apple and citrus flavours and aromas. Oaked chardonnay comes from southern Burgundy (Chassagne-Montrachet, Meursault, Puligny-Montrachet), California, Australia, Chile and South Africa. Aromas are bold, rich, buttery and nutty, with sweet vanilla tones. Acidity is lower in these wines. The palate is rich and creamy, with ripe melon and nut flavours.

Match with: *oaked* – cheese, poultry, white fish, lobster, salmon, shellfish, veal. *Unoaked* – cheese dishes, simply cooked fish, shellfish.

Chenin Blanc

A steely, dry wine with high acidity. The palate has flavours of apples, apricots and honey with nutty overtones. The best examples are found in the Loire, e.g. Savennières, where wines develop fantastic complexity with ageing. South Africa produces some good examples for earlier drinking.

Match with: goat's cheese, fish, poultry, shellfish, risotto, spicy food, pâtés.

Gewürztraminer

Striking aromas of lychees, roses and Turkish delight. Flavours are flowery and spicy, with lychees, ginger and cinnamon. Acidity is low and wines are best drunk young. The best examples are from Alsace, Austria and Germany.

Match with: sole or vegetables, or drink as an aperitif.

Pinot Gris/Pinot Grigio

Spicy aromas with a floral background. Flavours on the palate are rich, peachy and spicy in Alsace, Germany and Austria, with medium acidity. Wines are drier, lighter, crisper and not so aromatic in northern Italy. The best examples come from Alsace, Germany, Austria and Italy; new plantings reflect Pinot Grigio's growing popularity in California.

Match with: John Dory, ray.

Riesling

One of the most underated grapes, Riesling is an ideal food wine because of its naturally high acidity. Dry Rieslings from Germany, Alsace and Austria are aromatic and flowery, with citrus aromas and a mineral edge. Grapefruit and citrus flavours dominate the palate. New World Rieslings (Australia, New Zealand) are higher in alcohol, are fuller bodied and have richer fruit, very often with a strong lime element.

Match with: fish, duck, goose, ham, salmon, smoked fish.

Sauvignon Blanc

Aromatic grape with high acidity. Grassy aromas, gooseberries, sometimes hints of asparagus. High acidity on the palate and delicious flinty flavours, gooseberry and citrus. Best Old World examples are from the Loire (Sancerre, Pouilly-Fumé), Bordeaux (white Graves) and Rueda in Spain. The best New World Sauvignons are from New Zealand, South Africa and the Margaret River area of Australia. Fumé blanc is the Californian version.

Match with: goat's cheese, tomato sauce, crab, fish, shellfish, smoked salmon.

Sémillon

Often blended with Sauvignon Blanc in Bordeaux. Waxy, toasty aromas, low acidity. Richly textured, with honey and nuts, Sémillon produces full-flavoured wines that are often oaked. Young Australian oaked examples are richer in fruit, with apricot and mango flavours. Very long lived. The best examples come from Australia's Hunter Valley and Bordeaux.

Match with: shellfish, fish, poultry.

Dry reds

Cabernet Sauvignon and blends

A Bordeaux grape, but now planted worldwide. Aromas of blackcurrants, black fruits and cedar in the Old World, eucalyptus and mint in the New. Very tannic, benefits from ageing in oak barrels. The best examples hail from Bordeaux, California, Australia, South Africa and Chile, and are often blended, mainly with Merlot and Cabernet Franc. Benefits from long ageing.

Match with: hard cheese, red meats, duck, venison.

Merlot

Soft, ripe and plummy, with damson and fruit cake aromas. A fleshy wine, with flavours of fruits of the forest, plums and damsons, it has soft tannins and a delicious, velvety texture. The best examples come from St Emilion and Pomerol, where it is often blended with Cabernet Sauvignon, and California. Also found in Australia, South Africa and Chile.

Match with: duck, lamb, game.

Pinot Noir

A pale wine, but with plenty of aroma and fruit. Depending on where it comes from, aromas are of strawberries, black cherries and violets. When aged, it takes on nuances of mushrooms and truffles – even a whiff of the farmyard. Pinot Noir has a silky, velvety texture and flavours of black cherries, strawberries and sometimes a little spice. Although it's a less tannic grape variety than Cabernet Sauvignon, it benefits from long ageing. Best examples are from Burgundy; also found in California (Carneros), Oregon, South Africa and New Zealand.

Match with: salmon, tuna, meaty white fish, duck, game, goose, beef, ham, roast poultry, veal, mushrooms.

Sangiovese

One of Italy's stars. Aromas of cherries and cold tea, with flavours of cherries and plums. Acidity is high, as are tannins; wines age very well. The most outstanding wines are Chianti and Brunello di Montalcino; Sangiovese is blended with Cabernet Sauvignon in Supertuscan wines. Also found in California.

Match with: pasta dishes, beef, pork, turkey, veal.

Syrah/Shiraz

Known as Syrah in the Old World and Shiraz in the New. Spicy, black fruit aromas with leather developing in mature wines. Flavours are intense and even tarry – blackberries, spice, chocolate. Firm tannins often need time to soften. The best examples come from the northern Rhône (Hermitage, Côte-Rôtie). It is blended in the southern Rhône (Châteauneuf-du-Pape); in the New World, Australia and South Africa produce excellent Shiraz.

Match with: duck, goose, game, turkey, beef, wild mushrooms.

Tempranillo

Spicy aromas with cooked strawberries and a hint of tobacco, but with a certain complexity. Acidity and tannin are on the low side; wines are broad, rich and expressive and can be drunk young (crianza), when they are light and fruity, or older (reserva or gran reserva), when wines from the best years develop a wonderful complexity and maturity. Mainstay of Rioja and Ribera del Duero, but widespread in the rest of Spain; known as Tinta Roriz in Portugal.

Match with: game, poultry, lamb, mushrooms, truffles.

Rosé

Dry rosé wines are flexible when it comes to food. Good examples have plenty of red fruit on the palate and lively acidity. Rosé is made all over the world.

Match with: shellfish, fish, poultry or cold meats, or drink as an aperitif.

Sweet wines

Chenin Blanc

Very susceptible to botrytis, which intensifies sweetness and flavour. With honey and barley sugar aromas, flavours are of peach, barley sugar and marzipan. Chenin Blanc has a wonderful backbone of acidity, which keeps the wine fresh and light. Wines will improve and mature for decades. Best examples are from the Loire Valley – Vouvray, Coteaux du Layon, Bonnezeaux, Quarts de Chaume.

Match with: fruit-based puddings, white chocolate.

Riesling

Wonderful ageing ability due to its very high acidity and fruit extract. Young Riesling has citrus and grapefruit aromas, but the best Rieslings are mature, when they develop a definite whiff of kerosene and take on honey and apricot nuances. The palate is full of peach, honey, apricot and passion fruit. Length is memorable. Best examples are late-harvest wines from Germany, Austria and Alsace.

Match with: foie gras, fruit-based puddings, custards, ice cream.

Sémillon

Usually blended with Sauvignon Blanc and Muscadelle; wines are often affected by botrytis. Honeysuckle and orange aromas and deliciously waxy, creamy flavours of honey, nectarines and marmalade. Acidity is balanced by the presence of Sauvignon Blanc. These wines can live for many years. The best examples are from Bordeaux, e.g. Sauternes, Barsac, Monbazillac. The most famous sweet wine in the world, Château d'Yquem, is a Sauternes.

Match with: blue cheese, foie gras, custard puddings.

Tokaji

Famous sweet Hungarian wine made with the Furmint grape, which is high in sugar, acidity and fruit. It is also very susceptible to noble rot, which adds complexity. Wonderful ageing potential. Apricot, orange and marzipan flavours, with nutty spiciness veering to cinnamon in aged examples, vibrant acidity and a long, smoky finish.

Match with: blue cheese, foie gras, Christmas pudding, rich desserts.

Fortified wines

Port

Tawny: Aged in wood, normally a blend of several vintages. Tawny in colour, it has a silky texture and a lovely spicy, nutty character.

Late-bottled vintage: Wine from a single year, aged in cask and bottled after 4–6 years. Prunes, plums, spice and Christmas cake flavours. Good examples give vintage port a run for its money.

Vintage: Wine from the best vineyards, made only in 'declared' (excellent) years. Aged in bottle rather than cask, it throws a deposit of sediment and has to be decanted. Blackberries, black cherries, mulberries and figs, with an abundance of cinnamon and fruit cake. Tannins can be firm in youth, but become yielding and velvety with age.

Match with: Stilton, Cheddar, chocolate desserts, nuts, or on its own after dinner.

Sherry

Manzanilla: Pale in colour, delicate, with a salty, nutty tang.

Match with: tapas, or drink as an aperitif.

Fino: Pale, light. Rounded, very dry, almond and yeast aromas, almond and marzipan flavours, nutty finish.

Match with: tapas, or drink as an aperitif.

Amontillado: Caramel, walnuts, fig and apricot aromas. Rich palate, figs, baked caramel, layered and concentrated. Nutty finish.

Match with: *dry* – consommé, olives, almonds, tapas; *sweet* – trifle.

Oloroso: Burnt sugar and fig aromas. Sweet, rich, figgy, soft toffee palate. Long, harmonious, rich finish.

Match with: chocolate, custard desserts, trifle.

Pedro Ximénez: Dark and luscious, burnt toffee and spice aromas. Treacle toffee palate, very sweet, dark chocolate, a little spice.

Match with: chocolate, fudge; excellent poured over ice cream.

Champagne and sparkling wine

Non-vintage champagne

Champagne is made only in the Champagne area of France from Pinot Noir, Chardonnay and Pinot Meunier. Non-vintage champagne varies according to which grape varieties are used, but when young, it has fresh citrus aromas that develop a toastiness with age. With its crisp acidity and lively fruit flavours, non-vintage champagne is versatile with food.

Match with: *Brut (dry)* – aperitif, oysters, smoked salmon; *rosé*: shellfish, or drink as an aperitif; *demi-sec*: fruit desserts.

Vintage champagne

Made only in the best years, vintage champagne is richer than non-vintage, with delicious biscuity aromas. Champagne's vibrant acidity balances the rich fruit and biscuit flavours of the palate.

Match with: lobster, smoked salmon.

Cava

Cava, from the Penedès region of Spain, is made in the same way as champagne, but uses different grape varieties – Macabéo, Parellada and Xarel-lo. Cava has a different aroma from champagne, with hints of burnt earth. It's crisp and clean, with flavours ranging from lemon to biscuit. Lively acidity.

Match with: shellfish or Asian cuisine, or drink as an aperitif.

Prosecco

From the Veneto region of Italy, a light, easy-drinking sparkling wine with fruity aromas and flavours.

Match with: shellfish, or drink as an aperitif.

Asti

Italy's most popular sparkling wine comes from Piedmont. Light, off-dry, fruity, it must be drunk young and fresh.

Match with: light desserts, or drink as an aperitif.

New World sparkling wine

'Traditional-method' (same method as champagne) sparkling wine is made in all the New World countries, but the most successful examples come from New Zealand and California, with Australia and South Africa hard on their heels.

Match with: shellfish or fish, or drink as an aperitif.

English sparkling wine

The same chalky soils of Champagne are also found in south-east England, where some very respectable sparkling wines are being produced. Nyetimber is the outstanding example.

Match with: shellfish, smoked salmon or poultry, or drink as an aperitif.

Index